HER SENIOR YEAR - THE MOST IMPORTANT YEAR IN A TEENAGERS LIFE, THROUGH THE EYES OF A DAD

The Most Important Year
In A Teenagers Life
Through The Eyes Of A
Dad

by
Andy Smith

copyright 2019 TKR Publishing 2019 * all rights reserved

Book cover by Berta Martinez

Dedication

To Teachers Everywhere
The Most Important Profession
And The Least Appreciated

Introduction

It may well be the most important year of your life. So many of them are. But there are few thresholds that we cross which have more impact on our lives than this one moment in time.

Even with all the changes in our world, this one year has always been, and will certainly always be, one of life's greatest adventures as we try to figure out who we are, what we stand for and in what direction we are headed. This year is my daughter's senior year in high school.

Oh the memories of diaper duty, kissing owies, negotiating dresses on Barbie dolls, playing Santa Clause, Tooth Fairy, Easter Bunny, Mr. Nice Guy, Mr. Bad Guy, launch pad at the pool, and of course, Mr. Taxi man, all remain fresh in my heart as if they only occurred yesterday. This is what leads all parents to that one question that truly signals the passage into middle age; WHERE DOES THE TIME GO?

We only have three roads to travel in life. You can constantly travel down the road that looks back at yesterday and ask where has the time gone. You can ride the road of worrying about tomorrow by grabbing every opportunity that gives you an advantage in your ever frantic quest of building an uncertain future. Or you can mosey down the road of the here-and-now, understanding that life was not meant to be stuck on yesterday's memories or fueled by concerns for an uncertain tomorrow, but lived today, embracing every adventure that comes along. Though we all have a measure of each, I have always tried to keep my road of life traveling down the latter.

I have truly enjoyed all the memories we have come to know as yesterday, and have total faith that we will create an even better tomorrow. But today is today and it remains the only day that we have any control of.

So on this day, as I watch the torch being passed to my daughter's class proclaiming them seniors of Hillwood High, I take hold of my fragile heart. These kids will be traveling down the final road of their youth and headed for that one day that has always been the biggest day for young people for generations; Graduation day.

My daughter is a senior – and I am a senior's dad.

Where does the time go?!?!

CONTENTS

INTRODUCTION
  CLASS RINGS
  CHOOSING A COLLEGE PART 1
  SENIOR PICTURES
  REFLECTIONS
  FIRST DAY OF SCHOOL
  HIGH SCHOOL FOOTBALL GAMES
  HOMECOMING
  BECOMING A JOCK DAD
  GROWING PAINS
  SENIOR TALENT SHOW
  TRIMMING TURKEYS
  CHOOSING A COLLEGE 2
  IT'S EDUCATION, STUPID
  TALKING HOOPS
  HOME ALONE FOR CHRISTMAS
  CHOOSING A COLLEGE 3
  SPEAKING OF COLLEGES

Andy Smith

THE CLASS OF LIFE
REJECTION
SPRING BREAK
CHOOSING A COLLEGE 4
SENIOR PROM
NHS
TAG – ALONG DILEMMA
AWARD BANQUETS
BACCALAUREATE
GRADUATION
CARPE DIEM
FINAL THOUGHTS

CLASS RINGS

All Traditions Aside

Call me old – fashioned. Tell me I'm too sentimental. Say I'm out of step with the times. I will take my lumps where they are due me.

The first event on the senior calendar is ordering the class ring, and if this is any indication of what I am going to face for the rest of the year, I can only say that it is going to be a very long and difficult year.

My daughter picked up her class ring while she was still in the early stages of her junior year. That's okay, I guess, but it is my understanding that all her classmates picked up their rings periodically as they arrived at the school. There was no ceremony. There was no pomp and circumstances. There was no ritual. There was no tradition. You simply ordered them and picked them up on your way out the door when they arrived.

WHO CAME UP WITH THAT IDEA!?!?!

Sure, when I was a junior, we too ordered our class ring in the fall. But we received our rings together as a class at the end of the year! Kind of a ceremonial beginning to our most anticipated senior year. But that's not the half of it.

At the beginning of the year, my daughter brought home a booklet with millions of emblems, designs and styles from which to choose from.

"You mean to tell me that you can decide on your own what you want on your ring?"

"Yup"

"And you are free to pick any color stone that you want to have on it?"

"Yup"

"And everybody's ring is going to be different?"

"Well gee, dad, it'll have the school's name and the year on it."

"Oh, how nice!?"

Now I promised to myself when I set out to write this book that I would not fill the thing with the standard 'I walked three miles in the snow to school' commentaries. Actually, I grew up in San Diego, so that story has never worked well for me.

But come on! Isn't a class ring supposed to be just that!? Shouldn't it be a concerted effort by the entire class to choose the emblems and designs that they want to be remembered by as a class!?!

We voted as a class for one of three designs that a committee had come up with. When we ordered our rings, all we needed to do was tell them what size and whether we wanted a red, white or black stone on it – red and white being our school colors, and black being for those who were a bit too fashion conscience and frankly, made their ring look like a mood ring, appropriately enough.

It was a very important first step for a senior class. We had to make sure that our class ring would out class all other class rings before it. I am still confident that the Hoover High class of '70 ring is still the classiest class ring in the history of that wonderful institution of lower learning.

But now you are telling me that this all important first step in a senior class has been reduced to a serve yourself pot luck!?!

My daughter's school colors are green and white. Do you know that I have yet to meet a student with a green ring on?!? Not one, I'm telling ya!?! Oh I've seen some pretty blue, red, purple, silver, gray, black and white...but no green!

You know, I often hear people make comments about how our youth have no sense of tradition. They have lost their sentimental values. But I'm not all the certain that the kids are to blame.

When an obvious thing like a class ring has been

reduced to yet another big business marketing scheme with it's booklets full of do your own things, we can't honestly expect the kids to learn anything about traditions or sentimental values, can we?

I'm beginning to get nervous. I'm not sure my sentimental, soft heart is going to hold up well during this, HER SENIOR YEAR.

Why, I'm so upset I think I'm going to make her walk to school the first time that it snows!

CHOOSING A COLLEGE I

It's All In The Cap

Being a man of obvious power, influence and great wealth, my daughter is clearly on her own when it comes to choosing a college.

You're talking about a guy who's college transcript says, "Andy who?" and then quickly follows with, "You must be kidding?!"

Sure I went to college over the course of a few years, but I really don't think I received any credits for the classes I occasionally showed up to. I certainly shouldn't have. They wanted me to read too much. All I wanted to do was perform with my band, surf, and avoid a war in Viet Nam that I wanted nothing to do with. But reading books, many of which had very few pictures I might add? Forget it!

So when my daughter approached me for some serious

counsel in choosing a college, I gave her the kind of quality response that you would expect from a guy like me.

"College? Well....let's see...I guess the most important thing to consider first would be the location. The southwest is out. I can't see myself taking vacation time to drive through Texas or Arizona to see you. Now New England would be nice. I hear it is beautiful in the fall. I could certainly see us driving through New England in the fall to come visit you. Yea. anything north or northeast would work nicely for us."

Even though my daughter's face has that pained look of realizing that you have just asked the right question to the wrong guy, I'm feeling pretty good in my role of fatherly advice.

"Now obviously, the second thing to consider when choosing a college is the schools colors. I'm going to be wearing their caps and T-shirts for the next four years and well, you know how fashion conscience your father is. Blues work well for me...dark colors are fine...some reds, but not too much...and avoid orange."

Her face is beginning to sink to the floor in despair.

"And oh, don't forget about the mascot. There is no way you are going to Georgetown, young lady. I am not going to spend the next four years trying to figure out what the hell a Hoya is."

Well feeling like I have done my fatherly duty to get my daughter on track, I give her a big smile and hug.

"Hey, don't you worry none about all this college stuff.

Your dear old dad is going to be here to help you tackle all those important decisions, you hear?"

Her "Gee, thanks." wasn't very inspired, but hey, she's a teenager. She just hasn't learned to appreciate the value of good counsel.

For me, fatherhood has never felt better. I just can't wait to go shopping for my new cap.

SENIOR PICTURES

Getting Out of Focus

Okay, okay.okay! I know I said that I would not fill this book up with 'I walked three miles in the snow to school' commentaries every time my daughter cleared another hurdle on her final lap in high school. But hey – what's up with the senior pictures nowadays?!?

I took my daughter to school at our assigned time to pick up her proofs and listen to a 'brief' sales pitch that is long on mouth and short on heart. What a nightmare!

First of all, let me say up front that I am not a salesman kinda guy. I have a very low tolerance for those who sell for their wallet and not for mine. If I walk into a store and am greeted by a swarm of salesmen with commission written all over their smirkie smiles, you can bet the farm that I will not be making any purchases at that store any time soon.

Her Senior Year

I worked as a car salesman for a month before they let me go because I was too nice and too honest with the customers. That pretty much says it all for me. Just thinking about having to deal with another salesman gives me the willies!

So here I am standing there listening to this guy who's very presence assures me that I am about to be taken to the cleaners. He's got enough gold on his fingers, wrist and neck to pay off the national debt and the only thing slicker than his moussed-up hair was the smooth sales pitch coming from his mouth in which I didn't understand a word he said, but I somehow got the message that it was the best 'investment' for my little girl in this, the most important year of her youth!

The first impression I got when slick Willie opened up the gold embossed portfolio of proofs – hey, we just got ours in an envelope! – was, "My God, she didn't tell me that this was a modeling school!"

Eighteen posses in three different outfits with a variety of props and settings. Silly me. I thought that the guy was going to show me a bunch of shots of my daughter in a gown and we would choose the one we liked the best and tell him how many we would need and what sizes.

Unfortunately, like so many other things in today's world, senior pictures have become a high pressure, big business marketing campaign where the consumer becomes a helpless victim in a sea of hungry sharks.

The sales pitch is very smooth as the gold plated mouth

rushes us through the economy selections of token profits and skillfully rams us into the 'I can buy that new car if you order this one' package D. He just knows that package D will be a smashing choice that my little girl's family will cherish for years to come. With two more daughters to follow, I am certain that slick Willie will cherish his new car that I finance for him for many years to come.

This is a most frustrating moment for me as a parent. The rebellious side of me would love to tell slick Willie where he can stick package D. I'd love to get in his face and tell him what a slime-ball he is for taking advantage of a situation like this. I think of the kids who come from families that are less fortunate and how tough it must be for them to go through something like this.

But I have to turn away from my rebellious side and plug into the parental side that says that it's your daughter's senior year. You're not doing this for slick Willie, you're doing it for your daughter. You bite your lip, smile and refrain from doing anything foolish, even though you know that every parent in the room would testify on your behalf in any court of law. I politely made our choice and wrote out the check that I hoped he wouldn't cash for a couple of days and that was that.

Maybe I'm just getting old or something. I hate being in a position of not having any options. I can't tell the guy to take a hike and go get my pictures somewhere else. This is, after all, the only game in town, and no matter how much I hate being taken to the cleaners like this, there isn't a whole lot I can do about it. I come to a boiling point as I hand over the check, look into his eyes and see that he knows damn well that he will have every parents number on that evening.

Oh well, this is a very important moment for my daughter and I am not going to let my contempt for this bozo ruin it. They are wonderful pictures and I know that when we receive the final product, we will be happy to send them off to grandmas and grandpas, aunts and uncles, friends and foes.

I just can't help but think, however, that it might have been better if I had sent her to modeling school. At least then I would have some hope of recouping some of my losses on this. Typical parent thinking.

POST SCRIPT
getting back on focus

Well they came in yesterday. I tried to be stubborn. I was dead set on not enjoying them. I wanted no part in letting that slick Willie salesman get one over on me. After all I am the father, you know. It's my responsibility to stand firm, cross my arms and be strong in my contempt for this rip-off of our nation's children! It is my duty to protect them from the horrors of smooth talking fools like this. I have an obligation to set an example, don't I?

But slick Willie didn't bring home the pictures, my

daughter did, and the look in her eyes were well worth 1000 pictures. She loved them, which is saying a mouth full. I live in a house with four ladies who bring home school pictures every year with whining, grunting, gag-me-with-a-wet-taco editorials. But this time, it wasn't to be. Everybody in the house loved the pictures, and rightfully so. They were wonderful. And there were enough sizes and shapes to satisfy even the most fruitful of family trees.

I still believe that senior pictures should not involve several posses, outfits and settings. I still resent companies taking advantage of situations like this with big profits for them and few choices for the consumer. And I certainly pray that slick Willie's new car that I have purchased for him turns out to be a lemon.

But the look on my daughter's face as she proudly displayed her treasured work of beauty quickly turned the old man's stubborn, contemptible heart into a soft, embracing pile of loving mush. Why should I be surprised. She's been doing that for some seventeen years now. I'm not really complaining.

POST-POST SCRIPT
round two for the consumer!

As I have mentioned. I have two more daughters waiting in the wings. Actually, I don't think I have mentioned it yet, but you'll have to trust me on this. As I rewrite this book over and over, as a good writer must do, I can assure you that somewhere later in this book I do mention the fact that I have two other daughters, so go with me on this.

Anyway, as I do work on this book, daughter number two has decided to be a senior. This is a good thing, because I can throw in a few footnotes from time to time to give you a second opinion, or different perspective.

Case in point...

Daughter number two, along with some of her friends, decided to go in together and hire an independent photographer for their senior pictures. Oh sure, they still had to go through slick Willie so that their picture for the annual is consistent with the rest of the class. But what a treat it was when it came time to pick up the proofs and listen to slick Willie's touching sales pitch and simply smile and tell the gold plaited fool, "Thanks, but no thanks. Just slap this one in the annual for us, huh, big fella. We've got all the others taken care of. Thanks, again – Have a nice day!"

I was high-fiving my daughter for at least a month after that. And the pictures that were taken at the park turned out great, were cheaper and we actually got exactly what we needed. The lady didn't even have a package D.

Being that this book deals with school, it's nice to have a few lessons in it. The lesson here is that if you are a parent of a senior, you may feel at times as if you have no choice. You have no say in what goes on (see Class Rings story). That you simply must bite your lip and go with the flow no matter how much you may disagree. You must conform in the interest of your child.

If slick Willie takes good pictures and you have the money for package D, by all means, go for it. But don't feel as if you're trapped without any options. I'm sure there are independent photographers who would be more than happy to work something out for you.

It's a nice feeling to know that when daughter number three becomes a senior, I can honestly approach many of these events with a sense of having options. For a parent, that's always a great feeling.

REFLECTIONS

From a Surfer Dude Never Born To Be an Adult

Before I get all wrapped up in my daughter's senior year, it might be a good idea to reflect a bit on my own senior year so we can see just how good it can be. Yes, I was a senior in high school, and yes, much to the surprise of many teachers, I did graduate.

Oh it wasn't so much that I was a bad kid. Heck, I was Mr. Nice Guy. Everybody liked Andy Smith, teachers and students alike. I didn't have an enemy in the crowded halls of Herbert Hoover High School in the great city of San Diego, California. I was the kind of guy that fit well into every walk of life. The hippies, social climbers, suffers, nerds, the beautiful people and the dogs. The most likely to succeed and most likely to end up in jail. I was a welcomed face in any crowd. I lived by simple rules. I believed in having fun. If the atmosphere got too serious, Andy Smith would be the first one to hit the door.

I never judged people. Social standing never meant anything to me. I only worked on one level...eye level. Whether you were the class president or social outcast, football quarterback or flower-powered hippie, cheerleader or homely mutt – they were all eye level to me. I was a threat to no one and no one was a threat to me. I liked it that way.

School work was not a high priority in my life. It just got in the way of what I felt was the more important issues of school – visiting with your friends, hammering out the details for the beach bash on the weekend, and combing the halls to conveniently run into that babe that you know wants to fall in love with you. Schoolwork and I were never meant to be together. Sure, I gave them my attention during class time, but I approached school very much like I approached the jobs I've had over the years. I will punch in and give you a full days work, but when I punch out, my obligation is over. Don't even think of having me take my work home with me. I figured that if a teacher couldn't cover a subject in the hour that the school board gave her, I certainly shouldn't have to be punished by making up the difference by doing homework during my free time at the beach.

I was a young man with strong convictions back then, you know.

I did Just enough work to get a passing grade, but

certainly not enough to have much concern for where the honor roles were posted. I never looked at life in intellectual terms. The word genius was never associated with conversations about me. Nor was dumb or stupid, though I believe a few young ladies made a passing reference to the idea during passionate, well articulated rejections. I was a nice guy whose only goal was to have a good time. And during my senior year, I certainly achieved my goals.

Since I had already received most of the credits needed to graduate, I was given a choice. I could finish up and graduate early, or could take a bunch of dorky classes that have nothing to do with life in the free world as we know it, and graduate with the others in the spring. Of course, I chose the latter. Heck, I didn't want to graduate at mid stream. I might have to go out 'there' and get a job or do something responsible. No thanks. I'll hang around school and graduate with my pals in the spring, thank you.

So my senior year was a perfect match for a guy like me. Only a couple of classes actually required some thinking on my part, with the rest of the day being filled with classes that asked very little of me, to which I was happy to oblige (I am not making this up: me and a friend were the FIRST boys at Hoover High to take a Home Ec class! I learned to iron shirts and make tomato soup from scratch – and got a rather uncalled for attitude by the teacher when I pointed out that a can of tomato soup only cost 17 cents and takes five minutes to warm up). Simply put, my senior year was probably the most fun I've ever had.

Graduation day was one of the saddest days of my life. With so many of my friends heading out to the University of Everywhere all over the country, I knew that graduation meant having to grow up, get serious and start making plans on becoming an adult. This was not an exciting menu for a guy who's most challenging issue in high school was trying to convince the principal that being late for school should be excused, being that God created the waves and for a surfer to walk away from them would be disrespectful of what God had created the waves for in the first place.

There were many times during my senior year that I wished I could freeze time and preserve the moment forever. I didn't want to see it all come to an end. I didn't want my life to have a fork in the road. Graduation day and the parties that followed that evening were truly great times for me. But lying underneath the festive cover of euphoria was a swamp of disappointment and loneliness in having to see it all come to an end. I was laughing on the outside, but scared to death on the inside. I had no idea of what the future held for me. This was during the Viet Nam era, and I knew that if I didn't go to college, I stood a good chance of going to war. I may be accused of being a lot of things, but one thing I am certain about is that I will never be accused of being military material.

I knew that Peter Pan was just a story, but if ever there

was a young man looking for Never Never Land, it was Andy Smith during this time. I made plans for college, but they were not serious plans. Just enough to stay out of a war I wanted nothing to do with.

Now here I am a few decades later wandering down memory lane as my daughter embarks on all the exciting adventures they call your senior year in high school.

I'm glad to see that she too looks to embrace every moment of her senior year with a light-hearted commitment to having fun. But I also take comfort in knowing that she has also heeded her dear old dad's advice in maintaining a strong sense of discipline towards the academic side of the education experience that has better prepared her for life after high school.

Her graduation day may have a hint of sadness to it as mine, because she has certainly made the most in having a good time during these most important years of her youth. But she will also have a sense of excitement that I didn't have because she will be heading off to college well prepared to pursue her dreams and goals towards her future as an adult.

I guess that's what parenting is all about. You try to teach them all the good stuff that worked for you as a youth, and try to prepare them better for the pitfalls that you encountered in hopes that their lives will have far more successes than disappointments.

Maybe I have become a pretty fair adult after all. But please don't tell my heart.

FIRST DAY OF SCHOOL

Changes Come Slow for Parents

Actually, some of the growing process is in understanding that some of the 'big' events in our lives become uneventful routines through the years.

This is one of those moments.

When you are raising teenagers, there are many times when parents find themselves frozen in the midst of emotional overkill that are met by rolling eyes and comments like, "Oh, please", or simply, "Dad – dy".

This too, is one of those moments.

Now silly me, I thought that the first day of your senior year would be a big deal. A moment of great magnitude and scope. The beginning of the end. A 'Gentlemen, start your engines' kinda deal.

I stand corrected -This, I will point out, will be an on-going theme in this book. You will hear me say several times, 'I stand corrected'. The truth of the matter is that as a parent of teenagers, I stand for many things, but mostly I stand corrected.

I forget that we are talking about a teenager here. She sees the first day of school as the end of summer vacation, having to get up at 5:30 instead of 11:00, the start of wrestling with counselors to get her schedule right, new teachers and new subjects to contend with for the next nine months. Needless to say, on this morning our enthusiasm did not find a common ground.

That's just a part of parenting that parents never quite get. We are so slow to change with the times. I don't know how many times I've tried to be a firm, rigid, 'you're gonna thank me later' kind of dad when a voice in the back of my head plows through this maze of noble intentions and smacks common sense upside my head with, "She's not a little girl anymore, you fool!". Of course, she is standing there with that pained look with "oh, please" written all over it.

We parents get started okay. We set up a bunch of rules and regulations that are appropriate and follow the volumes of 'Parenting your way to Heaven' books that you bought when they were born. The problem is that those rules and regulations remain until they are ten, eleven… well, until that voice smacks you upside the head and reminds you that your children are actually getting on with life and may require a little movement on those rules and regulations that you hold on to so firmly. This first day of school stuff is certainly a case in point.

When our kids were younger, the first day of school was truly a big event. There were new school clothes, tons of fresh paper, pencils, rulers, folders, lunch boxes and what not. There were my infamous night before sermon proclaiming all the rules, expectations and fatherly pep talk for the girls to give it their all in all. And of course, there were the mandatory first day of school picture.

Unfortunately, we parents have a hard time letting go of such rituals. By the time the girls reached high school, these rituals and emotional moments had really lost a lot of their significance. And when they become seniors, boy let me tell you, these moments have about as much impact as sending a roll of quarters to Uncle Sam to help balance the national debt.

For me, this first day of her senior year was a big moment. This was the first day of the most important year of her early youth. I was pumped up and excited. My enthusiasm was overwhelming.

For my daughter, it was simply the start of another school year. She has had so many of them by now, it just isn't that big a deal, no matter how much dear old dad tries to sell it. Her enthusiasm was under-whelming.

But this is her year. I'm a parent. I have many years experience to help me understand the importance and uniqueness of how your senior year in high school plays into the whole of this thing we call life. Sure I'm excited and anxious to see her make the most of every day during this, her senior year.

She's a teenager. She has a future of uncharted adventure ahead of her. For now it's just another beginning of a school year. I know she will understand it better as she travels down the road more.

So there were no pictures, no sermons the night before, she pretty much buys her own clothes now, and the school supplies have become a year- round accumulation.

It was a quiet beginning to her senior year, but I'm sure the emotional level will pick up with each 'last time' she embraces.

Her last football game.

Her last cross country meet.

Her last Christmas program.

Excuse me, while I go get a tissue.

We parents have a tough time adjusting to these changes, you know.

HIGH SCHOOL FOOTBALL GAMES

Warming the Benches

In many parts of this fine country, high school football games are a big deal. Why in some communities, the Friday night football game at the local high school is the event of the week, causing some businesses to pass up profit margins as they close up early so that they, too, can run over and catch the big game. (actually, I'm being generous here, because as I have mentioned, everyone else is at the game, so they aren't really passing up any profits and, in fact, are saving money on their electric bill, but that's not the story, here.). Bigger cities are not quite that extreme, but it certainly is safe to say that high school football games captures the hearts of communities, big and small, every Friday night during the fall.

Her Senior Year

I guess it truly is one of the few remaining activities available that still gives us a sense of community. We no longer have the ice cream socials, family outings or Sunday get together at the park. The friendly, neighborhood grocery store has given way to the cloned franchise 'super' markets. The local diner has been replaced by generic burgers at yet another fast food chain. And the 'service' station, where you once could get gas, have the oil checked and take some comfort in knowing that the good people running the station know more about your car than you do, has fallen to the high-tech mini-marts, where you pump your own gas, pay for air, no less, and deal with employees who probably couldn't tell you what a spark plug is.

Yes in many respects, the Friday night high school football game is the only thing we have left that gives us any sense of actually being a community of people and not just another manufactured, cloned community like all the others.

I have always enjoyed going to these games, even when there was no particular reason to go – daughter #2 has made years of gymnastics lessons pay off. She is a varsity cheerleader, so I am now back doing what I did so well as a youth…going to football games to watch the cheerleaders.

There are many parents whom we have shared the benches with over the years that gather with us. From dancing lessons, girl scouts, gymnastics, cheerleading, sports events, PTA meetings, open house, banquets, fund raisers and the occasional disaster that we parents always seem to simply take in stride as being part of the deal. We have always shared the bench with them.

They are the ones who understand and can laugh with me when I talk about that bum who sold us the senior pictures. They are the ones who appreciate the joy of watching your child perform cheers in front of a packed house after years of stadiums and recital halls with only a spattering of dedicated parents. They are the ones who know that the only way to keep your sanity is to never keep count of the times you had to sacrifice your own agenda in the best interest of your child.

You don't have to squint to see gray hair on this bench. Trust me, they have earned them and they wear it well. And though they look a bit worn and used, I wouldn't want to share my bench with anyone else.

And so as we gather every Friday night at the old school bleachers, it becomes much more than just another football game. We have sat on our bench and watched young people wrestle with the issues of trying to find their own identity through the various groups that gather around us during the course of the game. We laugh and share our own memories and anecdotes of how we served our own youth with so much more class and style, even though many of us were sentenced to being teenagers during the sixties – a time when America, lead by our youth, simply threw up.

As senior parents, we are aware that we are traveling

through the last chapter as a major player in our children's lives. We know that this year, each event will take on special meaning because it will come with the heading of 'last time'. If you could get a dollar for every time a seniors parent said, "This will be the last time...", by the end of the school year, you would be able to put your kid through Harvard. We parents simply take this sentimental ride more seriously than our children. They just give us the 'oh, please' look every time we start pulling this last time stuff. But on the bench, as we gather together each Friday night, we all understand.

We understand more than our children the changes that lie ahead for them after this year. For the past twelve years they have traveled down virtually the same road with everything being mapped out for them along the way. After they graduate this spring, that road will splinter off into many new, exciting adventures that will lead each one of them to their own perceptions of adulthood.

I guess the truth is that when we tell our children that this will be the last time, we understand that this will be the last time for us as well.

So many of these parents have shared the bench with me off and on since my daughter was in grade school. There is a subtle pause in knowing that after our children graduate, our shared paths may well be reduced to an occasional run-in at the mall.

I have really enjoyed sharing the bench with these parents. There are some that I don't know by name. There are some that I have no idea what they do outside of being a parent. And I am quite certain that there are many who would stand much further to the right than I if the discussions ever headed towards politics or world events.

That's okay with me. Whatever their name, however they may pay their rent, and wherever they may stand on the political scales, doesn't matter to me. They are good parents who have served their children well, and on the whole of things, that's really all you need to know about someone, isn't it?

Friday night football at the old high school. Our team always gives us just enough things to cheer about, win or lose. There's always enough going on in the game to capture any idol moments in our conversations. Winning or losing never really matters. We want the kids to try their best and enjoy any successes that may come.

But we will all feel like winners simply by having been there. I can think of no better way to spend a brisk fall Friday evening than to take my place on that bench with this group of aging, sentimental, over-reacting, clueless, rebels from the sixties – parents.

And being that this is the last time....please excuse me while I go get a tissue.

HOMECOMMING

We Had the Floats, They Have the Spirit

Homecoming football games are a nice concept, I suppose. I'm not quite sure if the idea came from a desire to have students of the past come home to celebrate their past and give today's students a sense of tradition, or if it was more a matter of it being the one game of the year you actually had a chance to win and you wanted everybody, past and present, to come witness the event.

I guess it depends on where you went to school. At my high school, our football team still holds the record for the most homecoming games played in a year. I am certain of this. Other schools throughout San Diego would look on their schedule to see when they played Hoover High, and that was without question your Homecoming night.

Our problem was finding a game we thought we might

be able to win to use for our Homecoming. I think we pretty much dumped the idea of winning and concentrated on our halftime celebrations with our parade of state-of-the-art floats, marching band and what not. Hey, our floats weren't those wimpy things that I've been looking at being 'pulled' by cars. Ours were self-propelled with moving parts that would even be cool at Macy's, thank you very much!.

I suppose if your school had a good football team there would be a different approach. I wouldn't know. We made our coach agree to call no time outs, no huddles, and no long, drawn out plays, which of course was no problem. I believe the Hoover High play book had only one page. It read... hand the ball to #24 and try to stay out of his way. Of course they didn't, which made our MVP every year I was there the punter. It was my understanding that Hoover High still holds the record in San Diego for consecutive years of only the punter on our football teams getting scholarships to colleges.

I know that it is customary to say that things just aren't as good as they were in the good old days. But I must be honest in saying that when it comes to Homecoming, my daughter's festivities were by far more superior than anything I grew up with... the exception being, of course, the floats – I go on record here as saying without hesitation that never in the history of man has there been a class that produced better Homecoming floats than the Hoover High class of seventy.

Her Senior Year

During the few weeks leading up to Homecoming, my daughter was not seen until 10-11 PM every night. From running over to so-and-so's house to work on the float, back over to the school to help out with decorations on the senior hall, then putting the final touches on the senior section in the gym for the up-coming Friday Homecoming pep rally, my daughter was a no show at the dinner table or any family activity that was silly enough to be planned during Homecoming week. We were reduced to leaving notes.

Dear Daughter,
Hi! Remember us? We are your parents and we were just wondering if we might expect you at our dinner table this evening? Please let us know if it's not too much trouble, so we can plan accordingly.
Your Estranged Parents.

Dear Strange Parents,
We're ordering pizza tonight at the school. I borrowed a few bucks from dad's wallet... will pay him back next week sometime...Don't wait up, I have my keys with me.
Your Precious Daughter.

So after a few weeks of eating dinner alone and getting to know the extent of my daughter's capacity for writing letters, I decided to drop by the school on Friday to see just what it was that had reduced us to pen pals. I must admit that it was clearly worth it.

In our ever increasing world of cut backs and down sizing, I am happy to report that these kids have not compromised in the least bit when it comes to school spirit at Homecoming.

Every hall was bursting in greens and whites as each class competed to show the others that they, in fact, were the class with the most school spirit. In an old school long ignored by those who hold the purse strings, it was so nice to see these halls so full of life and spirit.

It crossed my mind how wrong we have been in taking the creative arts out of our schools. Teenagers are very creative people and I can't for the life of me understand what we were thinking when we took away all these opportunities for the kids to express their creativity. My generation must face the reality that we blew it big time when it comes to passing along to our children an educational experience that encourages them to develop their whole being and not just their intellect.

As I walked into the school gym, it exploded with school spirit. Let me just say that people who suggest that today's youth have lost their sense of school pride and tradition have never dropped by their school during Homecoming week. The balloons, streamers and banners made even the dullest of deadbeats want to jump up and shout, 'two-bits, four-bits. six-bits a dollar'.

I only spent a few moments in the school, yet I felt so

much excitement in anticipating the game with all its festivities tonight. I could only imagine what the students must have been feeling after all the work they have done leading up to this big event. I was convinced that Homecoming week must be the most exciting week of the school year.

When it came time for the wife and I to head for our place on the bench, we were excited and decked out for the occasion in our green and white garb that only parents would be caught wearing out in public.

The stands were much more congested than usual. There were many new faces sharing our bench with the usual faces we have come to look forward to every Friday night. Some, I presume to be alumni actually coming home, and some, parents who normally stay home on Friday nights to enjoy the peace and quiet, but on this festive occasion decided to come see for themselves what had caused their broken chromosomes to be absent from the dinner table for the past few weeks.

I was immediately impressed with the fashion statements being expressed by the youth. Dresses, skirts, gowns and ties were all the norm on this brisk fall evening. These kids really put their best foot forward to make this a special evening. There was to be no dance after the game as we had in our years gone by, yet that didn't seem to stop these kids from making this a night of going first class as only teenagers can do. They took a mere football game and turned it into a magical evening.

The band, though small in number, snapped out its musical chants with a crispness I had not experienced before. The fans followed their lead with an enthusiasm that quickly brought spirits to a boiling point. The parade at halftime, with it's cars full of cheerleaders – one being the pride of this old man!, Homecoming attendants – daughter #3 being a freshman attendant, providing yet another moment of bubbling pride for this old man!- and floats, was all pulled off without any disasters – parents just think like that. They can't just sit back and enjoy watching the kids having fun, they always have to anticipate disasters, which of course, is the leading cause of gray hair, ulcers and nervous disorders among adults.

My wife and I quietly sat back and took in the whole evening. There weren't the usual conversations going on around us as in past football games. We parents understood that this was a night for the kids. It was their night to shine. It was their night to embrace the final curtain in a week of spirited festivities. We knew that on this evening, our role was to quietly sit back and enjoy taking it all in. It was not the time to upstage them or complicate things with the usual restrictions of being a good parent. It was their night to shine and a good parent knows that the kids will always shine brighter when you quietly sit back and trust their instincts to guide them through the evening's activities in a manner that reflects the good foundations that you have provided them.

It was a wonderful conclusion to an exciting week. The

kids had done themselves proud, and in doing so, they had done their parents proud.

Next week, our daughter should be found at our dinner table again. In some ways, things should get back to normal.

But in other ways, things will never quite be the same again. We understand that next year, she will be one of those who will be coming home.

I am finding this to simply be the way it is on this, her senior year.

And yes, the football team actually won the game.

Welcome home!

BECOMING A JOCK DAD

Learning To Enjoy Watching Them

Being a guy of male persuasion, I admit that it has crossed my mind more than a few times how nice it would be to have a son that I could pass along all this manly 'jock' knowledge to. Hey, I had this vast reserve of athletic know-how readily available that would certainly give my son the edge over all the other boys. Who else would be better qualified to teach a boy how to turn a double play than this old second baseman with cleat marks up and down his left leg? "Get off the bag!", "Get off the bag!!", my coach would always yell at me.

I've always been a real sports-minded kinda guy. I'm probably the only Sunday School teacher who can turn every Bible story into a baseball game situation. Whether my son chose baseball, basketball, hockey or football, I was confident that he would have the best guidance of any budding super star. Attitude is everything, I would teach him. Learning to be a crazed maniac on the field, yet a complete gentleman off the field. Learning all about focus, determination, aggressiveness and patients. Those unspoken qualities that are as much a part of the game as baseballs, mitts and cleats.

Certainly, having a jock dad like me would give my son the advantage he would need in this wonderful world of multi-million dollar career opportunities.

As it turned out, however, the good Lord chose to fill my life up with women, just to make things a little bit more interesting. Three little ladies that would keep me so preoccupied with negotiating Barbie dresses, doll houses and such, that I all but forgot about my original plan of a father-son, male bonding stuff.

I was okay with that, though. It didn't take me long to realize that I was batting a thousand in the game of life. Those little ladies stole my heart in a big way. Their embracing smiles and twinkling eyes could melt down even the toughest of macho tough guys, and I was admittedly, pretty much of a soft touch, anyway.

It was fifteen years down the road a piece when I finally got my chance to be a jock dad. My oldest daughter hooked up with her high school cross-country team.

Isn't that the race with a bunch of antique cars driving from New York to Seattle, I wondered? Why would a high school want to put together a team for that!?! And why would my daughter want to participate in such an activity? She better not try and hit me up for my old VW!

Wrong sport, old man. Cross-country is a running race through the countryside that covers a bit over three miles.

Oh great, I thought. Now what could I possibly teach her about endurance running? Heck, my limit was running from first to third, and if the third base coach waved me home, I would slam on the breaks and yell, "Not without a bus token, buster!"

But then I remembered all that stuff about attitude, focus, determination and gobbling up the competition. Now that was the ticket for me. Sure, I may not know much about cross-country running, but hey, give me a couple of weeks and by golly, I'll have my little girl smoking out the competition.

Well it only took a couple of meets to realize that all my inspirational sermons, motivational parables and 'one for the Gipper' pep talks served my needs as a jock dad a lot more than they did her. You could look in her eyes and see that it was her love of running, and not anything I had to say that was pushing her to become the best.

As she wraps up her final season in cross country, my daughter leaves a three year history of achievements that is impressive. After a history of never winning anything in girls cross-country, she leaves the school with three consecutive regional championships and a reputation as one of the finest girls cross-country programs around. Certainly, an excellent coach who had a group of young ladies with a special chemistry had a lot to do with it. But my daughter has a room full of trophies and awards, and her name up on the gym wall establishes her as the fastest distance runner to have ever put on the school's colors.

It's not the awards and trophies that will do anything for her, though. It's learning to be a part of a team. Working and pushing each other so that the whole team can excel. It's the discipline of hard work after school and during the off season while your friends are out and about having a good time. Setting goals for yourself and your team and keeping your focus on making those goals reachable. These are the lessons that will carry her through college and establish her in the career of her choice.

My daughter became a champion because she applied her God-given talents to a sport she really enjoyed.

I became a champion jock dad because I learned to keep my mouth shut and simply sit back and enjoy watching my girl do what she loves to do.

And she came out of it without cleat marks on her leg. What a girl.

GROWING PAINS

Kids Do The Growing, Parents Get The Pain

As a parent, you go through many painful experiences with your children. Okay, let's be honest here. I love my girls more than I love anything else, but there have been moments when they have been a real pain in the butt.

Often times, these moments come at the hands of tangible issues that parents and children have been locking horns over since the beginning of time. These moments seem to evolve from tangible issues that you deal with up front and personally, looking for some middle ground that will bring about peace in the world and let you get back to your ball game on TV.

But sometimes, they are no more than a part of this crazy process we call life and requires no blame, consequences or apologies. They are appropriately called growing pains.

There is that moment when you realize that your child is no longer an infant, but an honest to God little girl. There's no more diaper duty, no more playpens, middle of the night feedings, or burping up green slime all over your shoulder, (parental tip: if you have an infant, never, never, never wear a decent shirt around the house!) and when she has an owie, you can actually pull enough vocabulary out of her to make a modest diagnosis. Though you have, as most parents before you, been waiting for your child to get to this next stage, there is a subtle pause in realizing that your precious little baby is no longer a precious little baby.

Growing pains.

Parents usually hate it, because it always happens without them knowing it. In fact, I might even suggest that the parent is often the last one to know it. After months of anticipation, you suddenly get that wacked-upside-your-head feeling when you look at her and realize that she has already reached that long awaited stage. There was no warning. It was not marked down on your calendar. It was never mentioned in your horoscope. And never, never, never does it follow the chronological order prescribed by the stack of parenting-your-way-to-sainthood manuals you have invested a house note for.

Growing Pains

When they become less dependent on you and rely more on their own awkward instincts and untested nerves.

Growing pains.

Those moments when you realize that it is time to let go of one era in order to embrace a new one.

Growing pains.

But the truth is that the children usually do the growing while the parents do all the pain. Growing pains are always tough on parents.

You have been looking forward to seeing your child reach that next stage in their life and are truly happy to see them maturing in this great experience we call life. But at the same time, you know that with each hurdle the child clears, a parent must let go of more control in order to give them the independence necessary to survive the next stage.

Growing pains can take a parent through an emotional wringer like nothing else can. I have battled through many emotional growing pains with my daughters. But in this, her senior year, I have hit the mother load of growing pains, (parental tip: if you have a child approaching their senior year, I am happy to say that you have options! 1- if you have a crooked doctor, you would be advised to stock up on your supply of Valium. 2- if you are a product of the sixties, you might want to consider re-establishing a relationship with the person who got you those cool drugs, especially the ones that really mellowed you out, man. 3- if you are a member of the NRA, please put all weapons of greater consequence than a butter knife in a storage room in Nome, Alaska, and give the key to a right-wing minister. Trust me on this, the temptation will become great, but you'll just have to work through it! 4- Join every high-profile, goody-two-shoes organization you possibly can now. This will help in your defense in any court of law, and also up the price you get for future made-for-TV movies they make.).

My daughter has reached that point in her life where she is truly on the doorstep of total independence. At the same time, she still has to put up with a lot of rules and regulations never negotiated and designed for earlier times when she depended more on mom and dad for guidance through life's straight and narrows.

So much of her life is full of celebration as she embraces each moment of her senior year in a manner that will provide wonderful memories for many years to come. Yet there is that subtle attitude that creeps in every now and then that pushes the envelope in what has always been the comfort zone in child rearing.

The details are not important. Moreover, it's that age-old, tried and true world of challenging authority. It's not really a bad thing. We all did it. Heck, I still love doing it. She's not hateful, contemptuous, or disrespectful. She's just confident enough in herself to be willing to take risks in her on-going campaign for independence.

In many ways, she is absolutely right, though a bull-headed father would never admit that to her. After all, within the year she will truly be an independent woman. She will decide her bed times, her work time, her meals and her playtime. It will be up to her to keep up with her laundry, cleaning her living space, her finances, her schedules and the Jones', if she ever figures out who they really are. I do not hesitate in saying that she has given me absolutely no reason to think that she will have any problem in handling this new world of responsibility that awaits her.

On the other hand, I have to remind her that this wonderful world of independence is still down the road a piece and as much as she may not like it, we all have to live in the here-and-now.

Didn't we all hate it when our parents glared at us and blasted us with that, "As long as you live under my roof, buster, you're going to do what I say!"?

And didn't we all vow in our heart of hearts that when we became parents, we would never use crap like that with our kids?

And don't you just hate it many years later, when your heart of heartless hearts reminds you of all this in the middle of, "Well as long as you live under our roof…"

conversations with your own perfect bundle of broken chromosomes?

But in all fairness to dear old dad, I have to realize that I have two more young ladies under that roof that you can bet the farm are taking a real interest in how this battle turns out for future references. I certainly have to be careful with just how far I let this independence stuff go, don't I?

You feel as if you are constantly marred in this gray area where there really are no simple, black and white solutions. Each time we wrestle, she can see in my eyes how much I long for the days when life was so much easier. When rules were established without challenge, to have just enough freedom to encourage a small dose of independence, yet enough structure to provide a sense of security.

Then too, I can see in her eyes that she doesn't mean to be difficult, she just wants an endorsement of trust from her parents as she ventures out of the nest and learns how to fly on her own.

Growing pains. Appropriately named, they are the common cause of gray hair, ulcers and a parent's general sense of physical well-being.

But I also realize that they will also be the source of much laughter in years to come when the Smith family gathers for another Thanksgiving to eat and reminisce about the many crazy moments in our yesterdays when growing pains created such a stir in our life of adventures.

SENIOR TALENT SHOW

Now That's A Tradition!

When my daughter asked us to come to the senior talent show, I didn't think much of it. Hey, let's be real here. These kids surely won't have much to offer. After all, the creative arts have all but disappeared from their educational experience, right?

Once again, ladies and gentlemen, I stand corrected.

Let me start by setting the stage for you. This show has become quite a tradition at my daughter's school. Every year on the Wednesday before Thanksgiving, the senior talent show becomes the main attraction. Held the night before Thanksgiving so that the many alumni who are home for some home cooking can drop by their alma mater and feast on a menu of talent from this year's senior class.

It's really a big deal. Much bigger than anything I can

remember from my high school days. Actually, I don't even remember my senior class having a talent show, and if it did, it would have certainly been appropriate to have it near a holiday that featured turkeys. Then again, if my senior class did have a talent show, they probably would have pursued seniors with talent, which of course would put me way down the list of people to contact.

I'm getting off track, here, – this, too, will become a theme within this book…"Writers who constantly get off track, next on Geraldo!"

My daughters' talent show has become as much a part of Thanksgiving as turkeys, dressing and pumpkin pies. There is no need for invitations. Everyone knows that Wednesday night at 7:30, the old high school gym will have absolute priority over visiting moms and dads, aunts and uncles, friends and foes. This is an event of great tradition that I would be well advised not to make any other plans for this night in the years to come. Wherever the world of opportunities takes my three daughters, I am confident that, should I ever lose track of them, God forbid, I know I can find them in the school gym at 7:30 the night before Thanksgiving. It's a done deal. You can negotiate the turkey, dressing and pumpkin pie, but don't mess with Wednesday night.

I was amazed at the number of hugs and emotional greetings erupting every time the gym doors flew open and another alumnus appeared to see what this year's seniors could possibly do to top what they had done when they were seniors.

So there we were sitting amongst the festive gathering, waiting to see what it was that had kept our first born absent from the dinner table these past few weeks, – Yes, another ongoing theme, here. Parents going to events to see why their children have been absent from the dinner table for the past few weeks.

Parental Tip: It's a proven fact that God created take-out for senior parents. Don't get too stuffy about your senior running off and missing another family meal at your dinner table. It's great for the kids to be involved in stuff like this. Don't get worked up about it. Encourage them, order take-out, and go check it out when you can. I know you'll be impressed, as my wife and I have been, at how valuable these events are for your child, even when it takes them away from what honestly should be family time together.

As I mentioned earlier, I wasn't expecting much from the show itself. There usually is one or two kids with a lot of talent and fifty others whose only talent is in having enough nerve to get up in front of a crowd and embarrass everyone else but themselves.

Once again, I stand corrected.

It was clear to me that these kids really used their nights away from the dinner table wisely. The show was crisp and orderly, with a nice mixture of music and skits. The music was very good and the skits were wonderful. Even though the wife and I didn't quite get some of the inside jokes being featured in many of the skits, it was clear from the response from the alumni-rich audience that they were beautiful representations of the teachers and life at their school. There was also a slide presentation that featured scenes from the past four years with music and poetry that was a stroll down memory lane that left a healthy lump in my sentimental throat.

As we were leaving, I couldn't help but be impressed with the effort these kids gave in an obvious attempt to follow the tradition set up by the senior classes of years gone by. God only knows what these kids could do if we, as a society, would encourage the creative arts more in our children's educational experiences. Heck, when I was a kid, we had so many opportunities to express ourselves through a number of creative outlets, yet I know that my class didn't produce anything near what we saw tonight.

Yes tonight we have had our faith restored. This, as well as Homecoming week, has shown us that today's youth are just as creative and talented as the youth of any other generation, if not more so. They have achieved a lot and have done so with very little support from their older generations.

I'm already looking forward to next year's presentation. It will be fun to see all the hoopla created when our daughter comes through the door. I'm sure she, too, will be anxious to see how next year's seniors can possibly top her class.

Post Script: I can't resist in pointing out that my daughter and a friend wrote one of the top skits of the evening. Judging from the audience reaction, it was clear that the skit had several inside jokes wonderfully presented by a handful of seniors. Though she certainly has her fathers knack for the written word. I am quick to encourage her to pursue a 'real' life.

Post, Post Script: Daughter #2 also took a pen to her senior talent show, and like her older sister, got great results. Her contributions were well received and she even sang a song with a few of her pals. I didn't even know that the kid had any interest in singing, yet I was completely blown away by her skills. Just goes to show ya, if you encourage your kids to try new things, they will never cease to amaze you on what they can do.

Posy, Post, Post Script: Sure enough, Daughter #3 helped write and participated in a wonderful skit at her senior show. Being the youngest, she certainly has a way with not letting her sisters get all the limelight. As number four son in my family, I can't help but give a spiritual high-five to daughter #3 for taking on the obstacle of the food chain and stepping up to the plate.

All this talent coming from my genes – who'd a thunk?

It was a great time, and what a way to start the holiday that gives thanks. I have a feeling that tomorrow the turkey is going to taste better, the wine a little stronger and the pies a little creamier.

But one thing I am sure of: The Macy's Parade isn't

going to be nearly as impressive as it was in the past. Big Balloons? .... Big Whoop!

TRIMMING TURKEYS

In Honor of Granny Dot's Sweet Potatoes

After the great evening of taking in the senior talent show, I was certainly in a festive mood to sit down and feast on another Thanksgiving offering of turkey, dressing, pumpkin pie and all the other stuff that makes Thanksgiving a time to give thanks.

This Thanksgiving had that underlying, uneasy, rumbling like the beginning of an earthquake kind of feeling, commonly known to parents of seniors as, "This will be the last time..." disease.

Next year, our daughter will likely be away from home and need a lot more than just dragging her out of bed to join us for Thanksgiving supper. Though she is not sure where she wants to go to college at this point, she has made it clear that she wants to go away and see how the rest of the world lives. This, of course, is in direct response to dear old dad telling her on several occasions, "Go away to college...see the world... do all that stuff without your parents hanging over you." I go on record here in saying that I am now eating my words. My daughter may be ready to leave the nest, but the old man's heart is getting heavier with parental panic as the moment of truth draws nearer. I now find myself saying, "Well, you know kid, Vandy isn't such a bad place to hang your knowledge."

I thought it was also fitting that we had no other relatives to join us on this Thanksgiving. Both my wife and I come from large families, so it really is a strange feeling to approach Thanksgiving and Christmas without any plans of getting together with any kinfolk. This year, our last year as a family under one roof, we were on our own. It was ours to choose the feast, ours to choose the trimmings and ours to choose the days agenda. Just the five of us. And although I was a bit excited about going solo, I was also a little nervous. I have always known Thanksgiving to be a busy time with many relatives around to wrestle through the menu with.

Thanksgiving has always been one of my favorite holidays. Hey, I like to eat, so any holiday that puts the main focus on eating is a holiday I can get excited about. Any holiday set aside for families to get together, eat a lot of food, and give a thankful nod to this rat-race we call life really appeals to this eat, drink and be merry kinda guy. When I was growing up, Thanksgiving was the one day where we all put aside our busy schedules and sat down together as a family to enjoy another great feast prepared by the mother of all saints, my mom. With six kids running around doing what young people did in the sixties, (we won't get into that, thank you) the Smith family usually ate meals in shifts. Mom would make a great casserole, and if you were lucky enough to be around for the first shift, you ate pretty well. Anytime after that and you were on your own. Keep in mind that this was before microwaves, so if you were late, you had your work cut out for you in getting that great casserole back to life.

But come Thanksgiving, the entire Smith family would be present and accounted for with our appetites synchronized to the same time zone. There was my mom and dad, brothers and sisters, grandma and grandpa Smith and Granny Dot, my mother's mother.

Granny Dot would always bring her famous cheesecake and her sweet potatoes that mother would never let us kids eat. Imagine growing up in a family with a mom that would actually forbid you from eating the sweet potatoes. Go figure. But it seems that Granny Dot liked to add a little shot, or so, of her favorite beverage to her tatters. The operative word here being 'or so'. We could all envision her meticulously following her special recipe... a shot for me and a splash for the tatters... a shot for me and a splash for the tatters. Well, by the time them tatters reached the dinner table, they were so splashed, as was Granny Dot, of course, that only a seasoned veteran of many a splash would partake.

It wasn't until many years later when I was out on my own, that I had the opportunity to actually find out what sweet potatoes are supposed to taste like. Not bad, but after all those years of the great Granny Dot sweet potatoes, eating regular sweet potatoes just seems to miss the true meaning of Thanksgiving for me. Even today, in respect for my dearly departed Granny Dot. I continue to pass on the sweet potatoes on Thanksgiving. Somehow, it just isn't Thanksgiving if the sweet potatoes aren't 90 proof.

Mom was the greatest cook. The kitchen was hers. She would get the largest turkey she could find and she would surround it with an assortment of tasty treats that you would never see the rest of the year. Small creamed onions, cranberry sauce, brussels sprouts, dressing, home made rolls and, just for a flavor of normality, good old American smashed potatoes. Enough food to feed an army and the Smith family was a respectable army to feed.

Before we could dig in, however, dad would always go around the table and make each one of us give thanks for something in our lives. Mom was always practical and religious. Dad always over produced...everything was always the greatest to him. My sisters were very specific and usually a bit too sentimental for my taste. My brothers were quick, to the point and anxious to dig in. Grandma Smith was always thankful for family. Grandpa Smith who was never known for his endearing tongue hated this part of Thanksgiving. He would always toss in a token thanks to that SOB down at the hardware store that gave him a break on some screws he picked up there last June. Granny Dot was always thankful to be alive, which by this time of the day was certainly a valid blessing.

For me, I was thankful that I had survived another year without my oldest brother killing me, but Thanksgiving didn't seem like the appropriate time to bring up stuff like that, so I tried to come up with something profound and sensitive to the world as I lived it. I'm thankful that the Beach Boys new album came out just in time for Christmas was one of my favorites.

This year, it will be my family alone. I don't think we will go around the table to give personal thanks. That was always dad and mom's thing. We will be thankful to be together as a family, thankful that we didn't kill each other, and we will be thankful that we are able to get together and truly enjoy each other's company for the day.

Next year, there will be a place set for the oldest child, but it remains to be seen if she will be able to take her place at the table. Certainly, the senior talent show the night before will be a drawing card for her, but with Christmas right behind it, we simply don't know what we can plan on.

We will be entering a new life where family get-together will no longer be assumed, but painfully negotiated through finances, schedules and, of course, the broadening of interests in her own world that she creates for herself.

After this year, Thanksgiving dinner with the family will no longer be a sure thing. The only thing we can bet on is that, no matter where we are, or who we are rubbing elbows with, there will not be any sweet potatoes on my plate.

Granny Dot will always be one of my greatest heroes.

CHOOSING A COLLEGE II

Making No Cents At All

First let me set the record straight. I am not a moneyman. I have never been very good with money. I do not pretend to be good with money. I am the reason God invented CPAs. I'll have nothing to do with credit cards, I will buy nothing on time and the only way I will ever balance my checkbook is if I throw it on a scale.

So you can understand why I was not terribly thrilled when I got the dubious duty of going to the high school to hear some guy explain to senior parents all the financial wonders of putting your child through college.

To begin with, I've got to tell you that I just don't get this college financing stuff. Shouldn't we parents be rewarded for getting our children to this point in their lives? For the past eighteen years, we have stood firm in making them get their homework done before they turn on the TV. We are the ones that have encouraged them to pursue every educational experience available to them, and then it was us who had to fit these opportunities into our schedules so that we could transport them. We are the ones who have sold boxes of worthless junk to all our friends and relatives, who by now avoid us whenever they can, so that the school could buy a new computer for them to learn on. We are the ones who wrestled with times tables, looking up answers to questions we didn't have a clue about, and were nickle and dimmed to death with school supplies and field trips that didn't appear to have any educational value, but were great opportunities for the children, none the less.

And of course, when you are dealing with children from a gene pool that is infested with broken chromosomes from my bloodline, it is nothing short of a miracle that these girls would have an attractive resume of achievements conducive to college and not a rap sheet familiar to the juvenile court system.

So after all this, you are telling me that our reward is that we get to sell our house, join the government run Society of Workaholic Parents With Kids In Colleges They Can't Afford But Don't Have The Heart To Tell Them, and go to some silly meeting where a fancy Wall Street kinda guy can smile at us and tell us that financing our child's education is really no big deal?

Needless to say, I was not very excited about going to

this meeting. Frankly, I think I enjoyed diaper duty more, which certainly speaks volumes about me.

But once again, if it's good for your kids, a parent learns to bite their lip, try to smile and simply take the medicine.

So I get to this meeting and right away, I can tell that this is not going to be a good thing. This guy looked like he just stepped out of Wall Street with his crisp, pin-striped suit, moussed up hair and enough gold jewelry to put my kid through Harvard – Yes, I too thought this guy might be related to the bum who sold us the senior pictures. You know, this could be a conspiracy against parenthood by some left wing syndicate.

Anyway, slick willie the second started his presentation by telling us that it is easier now than any time before to finance a child's college education.

Well there you go. He's already started out by lying. It is ten times harder to finance a child's college education now, because now that child has to look into my wallet.

Then this guy goes into an hour and a half explanation of all the various options we parents have in a golly-gee manner that made me actually start thinking that my daughter might just be better off getting into trucking school.

He passed out this four-page application called the Federal Aide Application. He tells us that we must fill out this thing completely and send it in. After about four to six weeks of looking over your application, the F.A.A. will send you back a pink form with your 'rating'. Slick willie the second made it very clear that if you didn't follow the instruction exactly and fill out the four page application just right, it could set back the processing into a deep freeze. He also made it clear that without this 'rating' from the F.A.A., your child would not be able to get any loans, grants or financial aide of any kind.

Well I'm not stupid. What slick Willie the second was saying is that I have to fill out this four-page application brought to us by the same people who bring us the IRS, and if I don't cross every T, or fail to dot an I, my daughter may be forty by the time her 'rating' shows up and permits her to go to college. I reached for my antacids. After his twisted, tangled journeys of explaining all this, slick Willie the second smiles and asks if there are any questions. Well, there are always one or two moms that play the 'concerned' parent roll a bit too thick, who will ask twenty questions or so, we're not sure, because the rest of us parents get up and walk out after the third. They are the same parents who asked twenty questions at the fund raising meeting we were dragged to in the fall – yes, brought to us by yet another slick Willie guy, but I won't get into that. Most parents wanted to walk up to these super moms, smack them and yell, "They're candy bars. Go out and sell them so the school can buy a computer. What is so difficult about that?!?"

The rest of us, of course, wanted nothing to do with asking questions. Sure, we were more in the dark about how easy it is to finance our child's college education than when we came in, but we didn't have the heart to admit it publicly. We all smiled a lot and made some of those comments that senior parents make when they have no clue of what's going on.

"Hey, money is really no problem for us. We just came to hear this guy for some friends of ours who couldn't make it."

Group smile.

Group nod.

You're out of there.

We were all anxious to leave. No one wanted to get caught being asked any questions that would expose our foggy state of mind. Senior parents always seem to be in a daze. They walk around with a fixed smile, but seem to have that pained dazed look in their eyes. I swear I saw two sets of parents walk smack into the locked doors without flinching. I even heard that seven sets of senior parents were found the next day wondering the halls with a glazed look and broad smile mumbling, "Money is no problem for us… our kid deserves the best.."

Well, when I got home, I was all prepared to take my place in the doghouse. I knew that my wife, the more practical one, would want a full explanation of what slick willie the second had to offer. She would want to sit down and apply all that I had learned into a game plan that will get our daughter off to college on the right track. I was walking through the door with a lot more questions than answers and was just smart enough to know that this was not a good thing, (parental tip: if you have any children who are about to become seniors, and your marriage is on shaky ground, you have two options; 1- call it quits now, and save yourself a ton of grief. 2- have a priest move in with you for the next nine months to be readily available to give last rights.).

Loving wife: "Well, what did the guy have to say, dear."

Confused, loving husband: "Uh...well...he said if we followed the instructions to the letter, we should be okay."

Loving wife, who quickly realizes that the wrong parent went to this meeting: "What instructions?"

Confused, nervous, loving husband: "The easy to follow instructions in this four page application that the government puts out."

Loving wife who is quickly losing her loving status: "The Government? ...application? ...just what are we applying for?"

Confused, loving husband who is quickly losing ground and feeling a bit moist under the collar: "Well... a number... actually, it's a rating from the government, I guess."

Loving wife who seems peculiarly attracted to the knife she has been cutting celery with: "You guess?"

Confused, loving husband who is having flashbacks of all those movies he probably should not have watched about disgruntled wives plotting against their worthless husbands: "Well it seems that we just fill this thing out and send it in. After four to six weeks, the government sends us back this number, or rating, that everyone else understands but parents. The university, banks and government will use this rating, that we parents will not understand, to let us know how our daughter will be able to get through college"

Loving wife, who has now stopped cutting celery and clings to the very sharp knife that she has embedded into the cutting board: "What about the other girls? They will be heading to college too, you know... what about interest rates?... How long will we have to pay for all this?...What about scholarships?... Did you ask any questions?"

Loving husband who realizes that he has no more answers that will satisfy this conversation: "Well gee honey, I have an image to think about, you know. You don't want everyone to think that our daughter's father is a geek who doesn't know anything, do ya? Besides, the guy said that all the information is in this stuff he passed out. I'm sure it will all work out just fine if we take it step by step."

Loving wife with a very uncomfortable glare in her eyes: "Step by step is fine, but the first step was to go to this meeting and actually get some information, not just pick up a bunch of papers."

Loving husband who really wants to get out of this conversation: "It will be okay, I promise. I'll take care of the whole thing. You'll see. We'll get that kid through college, if it's the last thing I do"

The look in my loving wife's eyes, and the white

knuckles in her fist that still clings to the very sharp knife embedded in the cutting board, tells me that this was not the best comment to make at this time.

Post script: It will be noted here that the nightmare was just beginning for my daughter and I. We filled out the F.A.A. form with paranoid care and got it in the mail at the appropriate time. We waited and waited and waited. No word from our friendly federal government. My daughter went off to college with the university assuring us that they would be able to help us get that 'rating' from the F.A.A., and everything would work out. I can't give you a blow by blow account of the events that evolved from here. Let's just say that my daughter spent her first semester of college dealing more in the financial aid office than in any classrooms. I spent a house note in phone bills between the F.A.A. people in Iowa and my daughter's university, trying to get this matter cleared up. To this day, my daughter has never received her 'rating' from the government. She has been asked to leave the university, being that they are unable to carry a student financially for two semesters. The university blames the Feds. The Feds blame the university. They both blame me for following their instructions, I suppose. My daughter is now discouraged, waiting tables and trying to regroup. And somehow, I have been stuck with a four thousand dollar bill because it was my fault in the first place for thinking that an organization that brought us the IRS and another organization that gives diplomas to strapping young athletes that can't read could possibly perform a simple task as giving my talented daughter a mere 'rating', so that she could quietly go about her business of getting an education. The absolute feeling of disappointment, frustration and hopelessness in dealing with this matter has been overwhelming. I pray that no other parents have to go through a nightmare like this has been.

Post-Post Script: Daughter number two is heading for college in the fall. We filled out the forms and got them in the mail on time, just as we had with daughter number 1. The only difference this time was that I was in no mood to go through another nightmare with my second daughter. I waited four weeks, then I called the Feds. And I called again. And I called again. I was rude. I was obnoxious. I was certainly not Andy Smith, nice guy. I raised hell with the university. I raised hell with the Feds. But daughter #2 got her damn 'rating', and is in good shape heading into her freshman year at college.

Parental Tip: If you are a decent, nice person like I am, please understand that nice guys really do finish last. If you want your kid to get to college, you have my full permission to become as loud and obnoxious and rude as you have to be to get these things taken care of. Remember, you are dealing with a government and university system that, frankly, doesn't really care if your child makes it or not. They simply deal with over- stuffed, over-complicated systems that are full of regulations, numbers and nonsense. You may- as several other parents around me- have no problems at all. That's great. But if you do start to have problems, please understand that the only way to get things done with the federal government or university is to raise hell, and plenty of it. It's not ideal. It's not the way I like to handle things. I certainly don't choose to be a rude, obnoxious person when dealing with things like this. But for some reason, this is the way the world works today. Give 'em hell.

Oh, and yes, daughter #1 has finally got her 'rating' and is hitting the books once again.

IT'S EDUCATION, STUPID

Sometimes the Parent Needs To Speak Up

Part of the problem with today's educational system is that the parents are so focused on their children and their busy worlds that they tend to miss the 'big' picture.

Every night, we can turn on the six o'clock news and watch as Congress and the White House debate health care, crime, budgets, the environment, military, re-inventing government, and a host of other issues that are sure to create votes come November.

As a parent, these issues, though certainly important, pale to the likes of surviving another driving lesson with a child who hasn't quite mastered the idea of looking both ways before pulling out. But I thought it might be a good idea to say something here regarding the activities in

Washington. After all, no one has invested more into our country's future than has the parent.

No one.

It has become trendy of late, for the politicians to talk tough and take a hard posture towards crime, especially in response to the shocking statistics surrounding the violence within our youth. Certainly, it is not a pretty picture out there and something truly needs to be done.

I understand the clout that the media has with politicians. Come up with a clever sound 'bite' or tough-talk phrase and you can elbow your way in on the feeding frenzy of a media saturated with 24-hour news programming. Stand tall and say, "Three strikes and your out, buster" and you guarantee yourself hours of valuable exposure on CNN, political talk shows and the evening news. Exposure you don't have to pay for and comes in mighty handy during election time.

And the man on the street really gets into this tough-talk mind set.

I often hear people say that they would be happy to pay more taxes for prisons to lock up these no good varmints. I mean, people get pretty emotional about talk like this.

I have tried to join in on this talk, but usually get verbally mugged when I do.

"Yea, buddy. Hey, what they really should do is save the money and make the prisons as nasty and run down as possible so that these bums might not want to go there. Hell, a lot of these crooks take a step up in their quality of life when they go to prison. They should take all that tax money and put it into the educational system so that all children can have the kind of education that will encourage them to live a more positive life"

Well the look in their eyes as they glare at me screams, "What in the hell are you talking about?"

Then they usually say something really bright like, "Hey I don't have no kids in school, so why comes I have to pay mur taxes for em? "

Why is it that when we start talking about paying taxes, only education gets such a lame response as this? I use to get upset when people said stuff like that, but now I just go with it.

"Hey, bubba, you just might be on to something"

"You're saying that only parents should pay taxes for schools, right?"

"uh-hu"

"Gee, that just might work. Then only people who have relatives in prison should pay taxes for prisons, right?"

Bubba gives me another look that screams, "What the hell are you talking about?", as I continue.

"And only people who have relatives in the military should pay taxes for the military. You know bubba, that just might put things in the right perspective. If we have more people with kids in school, then there would be more taxes going to school. Hey, why don't we go grab a beer and draft a letter to our Congressman about this great idea?"

Bubba is no longer in the vicinity.

If we are truly going to embrace this 'three strikes and you're out' idea, then we must be honest enough to admit that as long as we deny our children a well-rounded, positive educational experience with opportunities for all children to pursue their God-given talents, regardless of social standing, financial position or ethnic blessing, we are sending our children out into the world with one strike already against them.

People say they want to end the youth violence by building more prisons, passing stronger laws, and developing a no tolerance policy. That is all well and good, and certainly sounds good on the evening news, but I say that the real answer lies in building better schools with more creative programs for our youth to take advantage of. People say they want to fight the drug problem within our youth by spending more money on more drug enforcement officers and technology. That's fine too, but I say let's spend the money on teachers and provide them with the tools they need to make the teaching profession an exciting and fertile area of growth for our children to learn in.

Take the guns out of their hands, you bet! But we are crazy if we think we can do it by throwing more laws, prisons and tough talk at them. We must put something else in their hands. A paint brush, trumpet, script, mound of clay, computer, machine tools, piece of wood, transistors, graphic supplies, and many of the other tools that we have taken away from their educational experience over the past few decades.

Let's face it, we have not given our children a very strong message of how important they are to our future and to us. If we continue to put our focus, (and taxes) on prisons, tougher laws and even tougher talk, while our children continue to go to schools that are cutting back because of financial restraints, we are kidding ourselves. We can only solve the problems of our youth by providing them with a positive, exciting educational experience that will help them to develop the tools they need in order to pursue their God-given talents. There has never been a child born who wanted to grow up to be violent. If they do, it is only because we have failed to give the child anything better to strive for.

These short-term solutions may sound good on the evening news, but how many prisons will we have to build before we understand that there is a better answer? Investing in our children's educational opportunities has always been the only real solution in building a positive tomorrow.

A friend on mine once had a saying on his office wall that read, "The hope of tomorrow lies in the optimism of our children."

The hopelessness of violence within our youth must be the responsibility of us all. Looking at how much we have cut back in their educational opportunities, we certainly have not given them much to be optimistic about, now have we?

TALKING HOOPS

Or In High School, It's Really Called OOPS

With the beautiful colors of Fall quickly turning into the tedious pile of raked leaves, we draw our attention away from the crisp Friday night football games and head indoors for a season of slam-dunkin', squeak'n -'sneaker high school basketball at the old gym. With winter already flexing her muscle, we welcome this opportunity to crowd onto the shaky bleachers to see what this year's basketball team may offer.

Now, I am not a big basketball fan, but I do think there is a lot to be said for high school basketball.

For one thing, they play in a real gym, the way I believe basketball was meant to be played. With those wobbly old bleachers pulled right out to the court, fans feel as if they are truly involved in the action, and rightfully so.

Your head quickly becomes a target of any misguided pass, causing even the giddiest of freshmen to keep at least one eye on the game. You just don't get that feeling at the arenas of college and professional basketball games.

Another reason I like high school basketball games is that, with only a few exceptions, every high school has the same line up.

There is always the tall, lanky kid that reminds you of one of those big puppies. Those big paws tell you that someday, he will grow into a thoroughbred of a dog, but for now he is mostly a clumsy mutt that poses no real threat to the eloquent society. This kid hasn't quite mastered the game as yet, but his size is more than enough to get into the way of the opponents and cause a lot of problems. And the occasional slam-dunk he offers makes him a hero around campus. My daughter's school has said kid. He's only fifteen, and already stands at 6'9"! (of course, being the typical parent, my first reaction to seeing this kid was, "I'm sure glad I don't have to pay for that food bill!"). He seems to have the tools, and with good coaching and guidance, he may develop into quite a ball player. But for now, he appears more awkward than skilled. He misses more plays than he makes, but the three or four super slam-dunks he makes every game drives the youthful crowd into a frenzied state of celebration and has turned him into a bit of an icon at the school.

There are always one or two kids who stepped right off of the gridiron and onto the court. These are the school jocks. They no sooner make their last completion on the football field before they are busy snagging rebounds on the basketball court. And you can bet that before the last three pointer hits the floor, they will be strapping on the track shoes and heading back outside. They are not super stars at any of the sports they participate in, but they are solid performers with the kind of heart that makes you believe that they would be truly lost if they didn't have a game to suit up and get ready for every day.

Then there are the guards. There is always one little guy that was obviously told that he was too short to play basketball who has made it his mission to prove everyone wrong. He's the real spark plug on the team. He's more of a nuisance than a basketball player. His job is to simply annoy the opposition by zig-zagging in and around the court and confusing the hell out of the defense before he hurls the ball towards the basket, where our friendly giant retrieves it and slams it through the hoop to the delight of the crowd. The kid may be short in stature, but he makes up for it by playing with complete abandon and can control the ball even in the busiest intersections.

The other guard is the sharp shooter. He's the one who seems to have a remote in his hand that guides every shot he makes right for the hoop. He's the play setter who can burn the opponent that pays too much attention to the big guy in the paint.

They all provide a great night of entertainment, and when you add the fantastic cheerleaders – yes, daughter

#2 has followed the school jocks off the football field and onto the court. Rah!, the enthusiasm of the pep band and of course, the many entertaining side shows brought to us by the inventors of puberty, the high school basketball game, I believe, is one of the best values you can find.

As I mentioned earlier, I am not a big basketball fan. It seems to me that the college and pro basketball players are more hotdog than sport. But at the high school level, you see a lot more oops than hoops. You watch kids who have played enough to make the game entertaining, but not nearly enough to make it predictable.

Our team won more games than it lost, which was nice. The big guy made enough slam- dunks to keep the gym in a constant state of euphoric celebration. The jocks played consistent, steady games. One guard kept the other team off balance while the other guard did his part by sinking a few shots from other zip codes.

All in all, it's been a fun season of high school oops and hoops. It certainly is a nice way to take the edge off of those cold winter evenings.

HOME ALONE FOR CHRISTMAS

When The Magic Sleeps In

Christmas has always been one of my favorite times of the year, second only to the first day of spring training.

As a child, Christmas was always great fun. I would get those presents that would take up the entire living room floor. You know, those forts with a million miniature Cowboy 'n Indian, soldiers with tanks, cannons and planes scattered about with firm instructions for everyone to watch where they were stepping! Being the fifth of six kids, competing for play space on the living room floor was fierce, and controlling the traffic through said play area was even more of a nightmare. You don't know how many times I wished those cannons had real bombs in them every time one of my brothers 'accidentally' rolled one of their toy trucks through my battle field just when I had everything set up for the mother of all battles.

In spite of my brothers trucks, model cars and ships and my sisters Barbie dolls and accessories crowding my war zones, Christmas was always a fun time for me. It was also short lived though, as my enormous battles would be cut off with moms, "Andrew, you need to clean that area up... Your cousins will be here soon."

Of course, these million piece battle grounds would always be half lost or broken by New Years Day and reduced to a dusty box somewhere under the Bermuda Triangle commonly known as my bed, being replaced by then, with my trusted mitt and bat and days spent out on the sandlot picking up any game remotely related to baseball.

As a father, Christmas even got better. As you travel through this chaos we call life, there is no better role one plays than that of Santa Clause for your children. The opportunity to play a major role in preserving the magic and imagination of Christmas for your children is something that a father will always hold high in his heart of lifetime honors. I am quite proud to say that my children believed in Santa Clause well after most of their friends, and I say 'phewie' to those parents who believe that good parenting involves a constant dose of teaching them reality. I say reality sucks at Christmas and a parent should encourage the fantasy of the season, not discourage it. Heck, the kids will eventually put two and two together. But until then, Just go with it and have fun.

"I'm not sure about some fat guy in a red suit flying around with a bunch of reindeer," I would tell them, "But hey, you can't deny the magic of the season. It sure doesn't come from your mother and I."

Of course, the girls were young then and I don't know how many times a parent hears, "Oh they're cute now, but wait until they become teenagers!"

Although I have truly enjoyed being the bigger than life, only man in my girls' lives, I can say without hesitation that I am enjoying them even more now as they travel through the wonderful world of hormonal holocaust, formerly known as adolescence.

Call me crazy. Guilty, as charged.

But on this Christmas I have been thrown a curve of sorts. The rule of thumb is that the Smith family packs up all their cares and woes and heads for grandma and grandpas for a holiday full of festive chaos, with every generation well represented from toddlers to blue hair specials. It is always a great time, and we spend the entire summer stuffing envelopes with spare change so that we can make the journey over the valley and through the woods, to grandmother's house we go.

This year, however, the envelope didn't produce enough nickels 'n dimes to make the trip, so the Smith family was resolved to spending the holidays home alone.

As the season geared up, I began to experience this

sinking feeling in my soul that required some practical counseling from my better half.

"So, just what are we going to do this year for Christmas?"

"We'll stay home and enjoy a nice quiet Christmas by ourselves." the practical one responds.

"But how does this work?" I ask, in a bit of a panic. "I mean, the girls are teenagers. ya' know?"

"They'll be fine. They have lots of friends, you know. Why, we probably won't see much of them." She calmly smiles.

"But I'm talking about Christmas day! It use to be that we would have to hold them back and at least wait until the sun came up before they hit the presents. But now they're teenagers who would gladly sleep in 'til noon if you let them. And what about the gifts? You know we usually just give them money and take them to the mall to stake a claim on some of those year- end sales. What kind of Christmas is that going to be?!?!" I am completely wrecked with despair.

My wife, who has grown use to my sentimental overkill during holidays, just blows me off with, "We'll be just fine. Don't worry about it!"

You know, sometimes I have a problem accepting my children's maturity surpassing mine. I seemed to be the only one in the house getting lathered up about Christmas morning becoming a much more composed, mature edition.

I was outraged!

Next, I suppose they will ask me to accept the Fourth of July without fireworks, Thanksgiving without turkey, Valentines Day without chocolate, Easter without bunnies or New Years Day without hangovers. I'm sorry folks, but Christmas just can't be Christmas without early morning chaos and bedlam.

Of course Christmas morning found me sitting alone watching the Christmas parade on TV, drinking my coffee and waiting for any signs of life coming from the other rooms. Fortunately, there were enough packages from relatives far and near to create just enough of the Christmas morning atmosphere I longed for to counter the three small envelopes of money that the wife and I had uneventfully hung on the tree. About half past eternity, life finally surfaced as the girls made their way out of hibernation and joined me for a rather delayed, much less emotional exchanging of the gifts under the tree.

In spite of my stubborn reluctance to accept things the way they were during this downsizing of the Christmas spirit, I must humbly admit that I really did enjoy myself. There was still plenty of laughter, anecdotes and hugs to go around and just enough presents to keep us all occupied well into the early afternoon, when we were scheduled to head for a fancy dinner at a local eatery.

My wife has often accused me of never growing up. I have often been found in the living room watching Saturday morning cartoons while the girls were in their room listening to this week's top-forty countdown on the radio.

But this year, maybe there was a bit more to it than just that. Somewhere in the back of my heart, I couldn't help being reminded that this would likely be the last Christmas for the entire family to be under the same roof. Next year, my daughter would need more than just turning up the volume of the TV to get her to join us around the Christmas tree. She will probably need airfare. Starting next year, Christmas will take on a whole new flavor. A parent knows that once the children start leaving the nest, the traditions and mainstays of the holidays will no longer be a done deal. From now on, we must approach each holiday with nothing set in cement.

Her world will expand to an enormous level of opportunities for her. Certainly much more than she has experienced in her first eighteen years on this great planet. As her father, of course, I share in the excitement and have encouraged her to seize every opportunity she thinks worthwhile.

But I am also keenly aware that these opportunities may well come at the expense of what we have always taken for granted. Though I know that her heart will always lead her home for the holidays, I understand that the reality is that it may not always be guaranteed.

Starting next year, the 'norm' for us may well be Thanksgiving or Christmas. One or the other. We are Smiths, not Rockefellers. We are starving writers, not

Stephan Kings. Money isn't everything unless you live in my tax bracket, then it too often is the only thing that needs to be negotiated.

As Christmas day turns into the quiet darkness of the evening, I find myself, once again, sitting alone in the living room, pondering the events of the day to the backdrop of some football game I have no interest in.

I can't help but laugh at myself.

I have taken a wonderful day of family celebration and turned it into an emotional whirl wind of sentimental sighing that, annoyingly, always starts with... "This will be the last time..."

I'm finding more and more that being a senior parent sure irritates the hell out of me.

CHOOSING A COLLEGE III

Applying Within

With the Christmas decorations neatly packed away for another year, I knew that things were about to really heat up on the fast track headed for graduation day. I had been warning myself that once the holidays ended, time would suddenly speed up to a furious pace, holding me hostage to that one phrase that a senior parent hates to think about... WHERE DOES THE TIME GO? Why, if I had a dollar for every time I started thinking like this, by golly, I could put my kid through Harvard – yes, ladies and gentlemen, this too is an on-going theme in this book. A senior parent, born with a wooden spoon in his mouth, constantly trying to think of ways to raise money for his kids college education. I'm sorry to say, however, that again, I could find no one who was willing to pay me a dollar for each time I thought this. Your family and friends can certainly be a source of disappointment.

The emotional turmoil inside also picks up during this time. As a man who openly admits to living by the rule that the only bad thing that happens to kids is that they become adults, I am aware that the thought of my first born leaving the nest and seeking her own world of adventures is certainly a disturbing thought that eats away at you like last night's spicy Mexican dinner.

Simply put, her graduation and going away to college will be a very painful time for me, personally.

Simply, simply put, I just don't want to let go.

On the other hand, she has worked hard in her youth and developed into quite a young adult. Her many successes are not only a reflection of her own skills and abilities, but clearly a result of good parenting and I should see this as a time to celebrate and embrace each festive moment with the pride of knowing that we have done a good job. I can always sit down and cry about it after she leaves.

Sure enough, with Christmas needles still being picked up by the vacuum, I am told the deadline for applying to colleges is quickly approaching. Being the act-before-you-think kinda guy, I quickly encourage my baby to apply to several colleges.

" Don't cut yourself short, kid-o. Apply to a whole bunch of colleges, see, and then just sit back and wait. When those schools that accept you start fighting over you, you'll be in a great position for putting together a financial package that will best suit your need to keep out of your dads wallet!"

Being the obedient child that she is, she was happy to accommodate me. The other night she came out of her room with a stack of applications and proudly proclaimed that they were ready to go.... as soon as I wrote out the check.

You'd think that after eighteen years of experience I would have learned by now the absolute first rule in parenting; never, never, never encourage your child to do something until you clearly understand how much it is going to cost you!

Forty dollars for this application, thirty for the next. Twenty five here, another forty there... this kid had a pile of applications that would easily set dear old dad back a house note.

This called for some quick revision to my original plan of flooding the market. I worked overtime trying to keep my composure and blood pressure down while I negotiated each application with some smooth talking that would make my slick willie friends proud.

"Now trust me, kid, you don't want to go to this school. They have an awful football team. Who wants to go to a school that will make your Saturdays depressing?"

Needless to say not all the applications made it to the mailbox. She did narrow her selections down to four or five that she really had an interest in and I gladly wrote out the checks. I then made it clear to everyone that macaroni and cheese would become a staple at the dinner table for the next several weeks and I didn't want to get any attitudes about it. (parental tip: If you have a child, or are making one, two things to think about. 1) do not waist your time reading a bunch of baby books that try to tell you how to teach your kid to walk, talk, roll over, sit up or go fetch. Children will learn to do all these things in their own time. Use this time instead to investigate all the colleges and find one that really fits your particular likes and dislikes as a parent, and then spend the next seventeen years brainwashing your child so that when the time comes for them to apply for a college, they will only think of one school. It's a bit dishonest, I suppose, and certainly goes against everything I have tried to teach my children about independent thinking, but if you're clever enough, you can do it in a manner that will make them believe that the whole thing is their idea. 2) I highly recommend that you stock up on those little boxes of macaroni and cheese dinners. You know, the ones you can buy for twenty-five cents. Buy them by the case now. They're cheap, you can chop up damn near anything in it to give it a little variety, and come their senior year, it will become as common place in your diet as antacids.)

So with step one completed, we sit back and wait to hear from the schools, confident that they will all be excited at the prospects of having my gifted child, (don't you just hate parents who constantly talk about their 'gifted' child?

I want to walk up to them and smack 'em. Everybody knows that all children are gifts from heaven... and I suppose sometimes gifts from hell.).

I made a deal with my daughter that when she finally decides what college she wants to go to, she is to simply say, "Let's go to the mall, pops." I will give her twenty bucks so that she can run into a sporting goods store and pick up my baseball cap bearing the name of the school that I will be rooting for during the next four years.

Of course two of the schools are pretty small schools that do not exactly create a rush of excitement in any sporting goods inventory, so this just may be another case of making plans with good intentions that may require some quick revisions later on.

So what's new?

For now, we are all set, with the exception of having to run to the bank to cover those checks. This too, of course, becomes an on-going theme for a senior parent. I am confident that every bank in America can tell you when a parent becomes a senior parent. It is during this year that your relationship with the tellers becomes a first name basis – (parental tip; if you have a child who is to become a senior any time soon, scope out your bank and try to develop a close relationship with a teller who has a child in college. Trust me, unless your name is Rockefeller, this been- there, done-that experience within your bank will become invaluable when they give you that understanding smile as they creatively slow down the processing of a few checks until Thursday when you get paid.... not that any teller would ever do this, of course. This is just theory. I would never want to suggest that any teller in our American banking system would ever bend the rules for a senior parent, God forbid!).

SPEAKING OF COLLEGES

Let's Talk Dreams

Before we move on to the snowballing events that will lead us to graduation day, let me take a few moments to get up on my soapbox again and say something that has been bugging me for some time now.

In spite of some beliefs, I do have some friends, and I do have a handful of relatives that still acknowledge me in public. I do not question their love for me, nor do I dispute the heart that delivers their counsel. However, let me just say right here that in the great complexities of challenges that we commonly call living, there is no group of people more responsible for killing dreams than our friends and relatives.

When little Mary tells everyone that she wants to grow up to be a ballerina, it will be the friends and relatives who will slowly smother that dream with a constant dosage of noble commentaries with themes of reaching for more 'realistic' goals, often times without the benefit of seeing if Mary has the talent to dance in the first place.

There is no question that our friends and relatives will be the most challenging hurdle to overcome whenever we pursue our dreams. This college stuff is a good example.

I don't know how many times I have heard my well-intended friends and relatives make comments implying that I shouldn't let my daughter apply to such highbrow colleges.

"You can't afford to send her there"

"You need to be more realistic and send her to a cheaper, more accessible college that you can handle."

"You shouldn't let her get her hopes up on going to a college you know you can't afford."

The list of in-coming artillery goes on, but I think you get the point. Where did we go so wrong in life as to make our dreams such a negative, unrealistic part of living? For years people have been calling me a dreamer as if I have some horrible disease. Unfortunately, as I look around, I can see that this certainly is not a very contagious disease. We are in no danger of an epidemic, I'm sorry to say.

For some reason dreams are just not to be pursued anymore. Our lot in life, I guess, is to compromise our dreams and fall into line with the rest of the same-old, same-old world of con- formity. How many people sit around during their coffee breaks and say, "Well I really wanted to be a (pick a dream), BUT... (pick an excuse).

Well excuse me for living folks, but my daughter has worked hard to get to this point in her life. She is neither a natural intellectual nor athlete. She has never been called a 'gifted' child. Everything she has accomplished is the result of good work ethics and a strong desire to excel. She has been in the honors program throughout high school and graduates 37th academically in her class of over 250 students. She also leaves her school as the best distance runner in the school's long history.

My daughter has earned the right to apply to any college that she damn well wants to, thank you very much. She has earned the right to demand the respect of any institution that prides itself in the pursuit of excellence. And as long as she is my kid, she will always be encouraged to pursue her dreams no matter what anybody tells her! And without question, pursue her dreams regardless of any price tag!!

How dare you suggest that I, as her father, should encourage her to pursue anything less! Shame on you!

As a parent, I have spent a lifetime watching my children do things that we couldn't afford. The fact is that they would have never been born in the first place if I only lived within the measly boundaries of what I can afford.

My uncle use to tell us when we were growing up that every one was born with a God-given talent. Our purpose in life was to find that talent and pursue it with all our hearts. Fame and fortune should have nothing to do with it.

My uncle was Hermes Pan, the choreographer by which all other choreographers will be measured. During the golden era of musicals in Hollywood, it was Hermes that was called on to make 'em dance. He did most of Fred Astaire's movies, Flower Drum Song, Cleopatra, My Fair Lady .... well you get the point. His resume is long. He won an Oscar and an Emmy for his work, yet the man never had a dance lesson in his life. He pursued his God-given talents with all his heart and became the greatest choreographer that ever graced the motion picture business. Hermes Pan was a dreamer.

In fact, ladies and gentlemen, if you look back through history, you will see that it has been the dreamers who have ignored their friends and relatives and made a difference in this world – not those who stood passively in the line of conformity and only made excuses for their dreams during coffee breaks.

So call me a dreamer, will you? So be it. Guilty as charged. And if I have taught my children anything, it has been to always listen to their hearts and pursue their dreams.

Sure, they may not reach those dreams. Sure, they may end up with more struggles and heartaches than if they stayed on the road most traveled.

But in this crazy thing we call life, there is no greater

tragedy than to see a person come to the end of their life having never pursued their dreams.

I can only pray that my girls grow up to be dreamers. Looking back through history, they certainly would be in good company. And if you ask me, which you did not, but being that this is my book, I'll tell you anyway, what this world needs is a lot more dreamers, and not cloned conformers.

My daughter will probably end up going to some nice college that I can't afford. She has earned the right to. God forbid we should ever get to a point where an application to college would focus more on what the parents can contribute financially than on what the child can contribute as a student.

So let the friends and relatives tell me that I can't afford to let my daughter apply to such institutions.

I don't listen to them.

I listen to Hermes and all the other great dreamers who would tell me that I can't afford to tell her to shoot for anything less.

Dream On!

THE CLASS OF LIFE

Some Notes a Parent Should Never Write

It was one of the toughest moments as a parent, as I sat down to write a note giving my daughters permission to get out of classes so that they could attend the funeral of a friend and fellow student. What makes this so difficult for me is that this is the third year in a row I have had to write this note. My children have been to more funerals during their high school experience than I have in my entire life... and I will remind you that I was a teenager during the sixties. Needless to say, this is not a statistic that a parent likes to deal with.

The hows and whys of these deaths are not important. It's enough to say that these teenagers died being teenagers. Automobile accidents, sudden illness, crossing a street or simply getting money out of a 24-hour teller machine. They were teenagers doing what teenagers have been doing for generations... living life to it's fullest. What is important is that the students at the high school have experienced these deaths during a time in their lives when they should be experiencing crushes on cheerleaders, Friday night football games and contempt for math teachers.

As a parent, I seem to find myself at a loss for words. You always hope that you will be there for them, especially through the valleys of life. But what do you tell them as they quietly prepare for a funeral for another friend?

Sometimes silence is the only conversation that makes any sense.

These are teenagers. They should be out there having fun. They should be embracing life to it's fullest. And though teenagers often get a bum rap, they really are the only age group that fully permits the freedom of life to express itself through their many awkward styles, trends and forgettable fads. We adults often bad mouth teenagers, but I would suggest that we do so with a healthy dose of jealousy. Watching teenagers express their freedom in a care-free world irritates the hell out of us as we are reminded of our own youth and our passionate exploits of freedom being gradually extinguished by a neatly packaged world of conformity and responsibility. We just hate it.

Teenagers approach life with a full throttle of enthusiasm. Death should never be a part of their high school curriculum. I'm not sure how well these students have scored on their SAT's, but I do know that they have certainly had a crash course in the lessons of life.

Life doesn't come with any guarantees. If you are a good person, it does not guarantee that only good things will happen to you. Life is life. There simply are no calendars with tomorrows on them, only an on-going series of todays. And it's not how often we turn the pages of our calendars that measure a person's life, but only how we fill up those pages. Nobody knows how to fill up the pages of a calendar better than the teenager.

These are pretty adult issues for these high school kids to deal with. But as a parent, I have learned over the past few years that teenagers are pretty resourceful people. Teenagers are probably better at turning a negative into a positive than anyone else.

Once again the halls of the high school are uncomfortably quiet, and will probably remain so for a time. Getting out of school to attend funerals has worn thin on the spirits of these kids. But with the support of their parents and their community, these kids will bounce back, doing what they do best. Once again there will be laughter in halls.

Teenagers are already experts at living life to it's fullest, but these teenagers will have a better understanding of how precious and fragile that full life can be.

As a parent, I can only hope that I will not have to write any more of these notes.

Post Script: I am sorry to say that this story did not end there. Daughter #2 graduated from the high school last week. On Monday, during the most exciting week of her youth, a close friend whom she had known since nursery school lost her life in an automobile accident.

When she came through the door around midnight, I could tell that something was wrong. She had that look that a father never likes to see. Instead of spending the night with her friends at another pre-graduation party, she was coming home from the hospital where her friend had passed away, the result of another car losing control in the rain.

We hugged.

We cried.

There were no words to be said.

Sometimes life can be so cruel and cold. This was graduation week. A time of great celebration for my daughter and her friends. Instead, she canceled Tuesday's activities so she could spend the day with her friend's mother and help her out.

On graduation day, my daughter was understandably subdued. The funeral for her friend would be just four hours before her graduation.

It's a tough call for a parent. On this day there certainly was a lot more tears than words. Nowhere in any bible does it say that life is fair.

But I was once again reminded of how resilient our young people are.

I left the funeral and headed home to pick up my oldest daughter, then head over to hook up with daughter #2 for her graduation.

At the graduation, she found her smile again. Her voice was gone, the result of cheering for each of her classmates as they walked across the stage to pick up their diploma.

The funeral, just a few hours earlier, was a time to cry and say goodbye to a good friend.

But this was graduation night. A night that she had anticipated for many years. A time of great celebration.

My daughter understood both and gave them their proper response.

After graduation, before she headed off for a night full of various parties, I gave my daughter a big hug, looked at her and simply said, " You certainly have covered the emotional scale today, kid."

The look in her eyes and smile on her face was all the words I needed.

Dad went home to quietly recover. We adults often times don't fare as well as teenagers on days like this.

They're cute now, but wait until they are teenagers.

As a Dad of three teenage girls, I can say without hesitation that if you're a good parent, you'll pay attention to those dreaded teenage years and find yourself inspired more than horrified.

REJECTIONS

My Writing, Fine – My Daughter, Oh Hell No!

As a writer, getting rejection slips in the mail is as common place as hemorrhoids and truckers, grease and mechanics, the Cubs and mediocrity, and Republicans and starch. Rejection is just a part of the writers life that falls under the category of sucky things you have to put up with in order to get to the good stuff.

You write your piece, then send out your proposal to twenty publishers. Of these twenty publishers, you'll never hear from ten of them, even though you send them the S.A.S.E. that they insisted on. The other ten will send you a variety of rejections, mostly to the tune of poorly Xeroxed form letters that have been used so often that they are barely legible – usually coming from the publishers who make the biggest stink about writers sending their proposals in neat, clean professional looking packages. Or some will actually just send back my S.A.S.E. with a short note that, had I not put a code on the envelope, I would not have any clue from whence the neat, clean, professional note was coming from. Of course, every now and then, the writer finds a 'yes' in his mailbox and the world becomes his oyster.

People often ask me how I can put up with a world so full of rejection. I simply tell them that it is not a popularity contest. I would certainly be in a fix if they all came back with a 'yes' response, which of course is why they have a strict rule with writers that you do not send out proposals simultaneously, which of course we writers pretty much ignore. I only need one publisher to say yes. Hell, I ONLY want one publisher to say yes. So until I have received a rejection from every publisher on planet Earth, I am not going to get too worked up about it.

I am quite confident that there is no other person in the world that deals with more rejection than does the writer.

That being said, you might think that a guy like me would be more than adept at helping the kids deal with the nasty world of rejection, wouldn't you? You'd think that my girls would be in good hands any time the tears of rejection begin to fall.

Once again, I stand corrected.

The other day my daughter got a rejection letter from one of the schools she had applied to. Though she took the news in her usual easy-going stride, her father took it in absolute contempt. I was outraged. I was horrified. I couldn't sleep. I couldn't eat. I couldn't BELIEVE it!

How could any university turn down my little girl? Are they not looking for quality students? Have they given up their desire to be the best? Do they dare suggest that my little girl is not good enough for their school? Did she suck her thumb too long? Did I not potty train her early enough for ya? Is she being punished because I couldn't cut her bangs straight when she was younger? I was a basket case.

How could this be? I'm a writer, for crying out loud. I deal with more rejection in a week than most people do in a year. And I'm not talking about the casual, 'I'd rather dance with Godzilla', type of rejection – which I've had my share of as well, but we won't get into that. Writing is my life. I pour my soul into every piece I create. I count on my writing to be my ticket out of odd jobs, bill collectors and worn blue jeans, (though I go on record here in saying that all the success in the world would never take me away from the jeans and Hawaiian shirt fraternity). Every rejection I receive shoots straight through the heart of my dreams. Any writer that says rejections don't hurt is lying. It hurts a lot. You just have to learn to live with it.

But that's the problem. Writing is my dream, my God-given talent. They can reject my writing until I'm eighty years old and I'll never lose sleep over it. As long as I know that I am doing the best that I can, that I am following up every lead I am given and continue with the belief that my best piece is the one I'm working on now, I'm really okay. I will only lose sleep and be disappointed when I give up on my dream, not when they reject it.

But reject my daughter, pal, and you're messin' with the wrong guy!

You're no longer stepping on my dream, you're stepping on my little girl's heart.

My daughter had a great high school career as a student/athlete. It's time for her to go into the world and find her own dream. I've been with this kid since the delivery room and I can't for the life of me imagine any school not being excited about having her hang around their campus for the next four years. Why it's enough to turn a peaceful, fun-loving guy into a disgruntled postal worker, I tell ya!

Rejection is a funny thing. You can reject my writing until the good Lord takes me home and I will never change my pace. I am a writer. I was born to write. And I will continue to write whether the world ever acknowledges my talents or not.

But have one university reject my daughter and I become a raving maniac, even though her biggest problem is that she's been accepted by so many other fine schools and must choose from all the exciting opportunities they provide.

I guess it all boils down to perspective and that age-old handicap of being called a parent.

Reject me all you want.

Stomp on my dream and see if you get much of a stir out of me.

But reject my kids, buster, and I start looking for your car, with evil plans of slashing tires and.... well, parents just get a tad touchy about their kids being rejected, ya know.

To this day, one of the most dangerous jobs in America is that of being a Little League umpire.

I sure am glad that my daughter has taken the news so well. She is far too busy talking to the schools that have accepted her to be bothered any by the few that have said thanks, but no thanks. And of course, when the flames of fury finally retreat, I realize that the school's baseball caps wouldn't look that good on me anyway.

Again, it was just a matter of principal.

Parents are goofy about things like that.

SPRING BREAK

The Only Thing To Break Was Her Heart

What's the deal with spring break nowadays? Call me stupid, but I always thought that spring break was reserved for college students as a means of taking a break from all their books, basketball games and Gold Fish swallowing, and head for the beaches of Florida.

Once again, I stand corrected.

It seems as if the high school students around here do a lot of their spring flinging on the sunny beaches of Florida as well.

Now keep in mind that I grew up on the beaches of San Diego, so this spring break stuff of heading for the beaches didn't really hold that much enthusiasm in my life as it apparently does those who have survived the wonderful winter months of wind chill factors.

But high school kids? At the risk of sounding like a parent, God forbid, isn't that a bit early to begin the springtime ritual of beach front R&R?

Evidently not.

Seems like heading to Florida at spring break is a bit of a tradition with the high school crowd around here. Yes, there are always a handful of parents at the ready to serve as surrogate nags, but still, it's a tough call for a parent.

This is when you hate being a parent of a teenager. This is the stuff that creates gray hair, bags under the eyes and male menopause. You become very uneasy at the thought of your pride 'n joy being any further than a short drive away.

But as was the case in all the other stages of life she has traveled through, a parent often has to learn to bite their lips and simply trust the kid. You have to believe that you have raised them to use good judgment in every situation without dear old dad standing at the ready to bail them out, should something go wrong.

You have to let go, and don't let any parent fool you, we just hate to let go.

So after much negotiating and hammering out the small details, my daughter headed for the beaches of Florida.

I really was okay with the whole thing. I realized that my worries came from thinking in terms of Andy Smith and not my daughter. I was thinking about me and my circle of friends when I was a brain-dead teenager and what we would do had we been given a week of R&R at the beach without our parents.

Now that's some spooky thinking that will make a nervous wreck out of a paranoid parent in a heartbeat, I'm tellin' ya.

But the group of kids that my daughter would be going with was certainly a cut above the circle of friends I hung around with. These are good kids. The kind of kids you never hear about on the six o'clock news. Though they are teenagers who certainly know how to have a good time, there is not one in the crowd that has had any run-ins with drugs, alcohol or anti-establishment type of behavior.

Hey, if you can't trust this group of kids, your trust level is in dire need of some CPR.

It was Monday night when I got the call.

A very tearful young lady on the other end told me that she and her friends would be heading home, being asked to pack up all their cares and woes and leave Florida.

Here's the story, as told by my daughter and later confirmed by the parents and others who were there.

The girls, six with two adults, had spent their first day checking out the beach scene and generally unwinding. As the sun became a sunset, they all gathered at the condo to prepare for a night on the town. It seems that a handful of boys from their school found out where they were staying and had dropped by to check things out. The girls tried valiantly to get rid of the guys, who had obviously gotten a head start on the party refreshments, but with little success.

Keep in mind here that part of the deal was that there would be no boys from the school hanging around. Certainly, when you mix babes and beaches you usually get guys, but we wanted it very clear from the beginning that they were not to be passing out their address to the guys at school, who have worked very hard at proving the theory that young ladies mature a lot faster than boys. This truly was not a problem for the girls, who were actually looking forward to getting away from the home grown variety and seeing if their might be any life from other planets.

I, for one, had no doubt that these boys were uninvited and unwanted guests.

Well it seems that these boys, whose behavior was unimpressive under normal circumstances, were even less impressive this evening. One of them very generously donated his lunch to the front yard. Security guards at the condo saw this and without hesitation, asked everyone to pack up and leave. The party was over.

What made the thing worse is that the boys got to stay in Florida for the week, being that they were staying at another location and, being the mature, responsible young lads that they were, fled the scene of the crime as soon as they saw security heading their way. What made it even worser (I know that's not a word, but I do try to speak their language when I can, you know), is that my daughter and a friend were not even there when the infraction occurred. They had been walking up to the store to pick up a few items only to return to a house full of tearful young ladies and their long anticipated trip to Florida abruptly over.

One could certainly argue that the girls should not have been thrown out. They did not invite the boys and were clearly making an effort to get rid of them.

But I certainly understand the position of the people who run the condos. We live in a world where innocent fun so quickly escalates into disaster, and I have no problem with understanding the need to nip such things in the bud quickly and without a lot of negotiations. After all, the rules were very clear when they rented the condo, which of course is why the girls tried so desperately to get rid of the boys in the first place. It may have been unfair for the girls to pay such a heavy price for the boys behavior, while the boys virtually walked... hell, ran away without any consequences. But as a parent, I will feel much better about sending my girls off to Florida in the coming years.

Early the next morning, a very dejected, weary young lady came dragging through the door. Her best friend was with her, a victim of being left an orphan by her parents who were taking some R&R of their own. There wasn't much to say in a situation like this. Certainly, any sermons or preaching about moral standards would be way...way... out of line.

My daughter was worried that she would be grounded when she got home. I smiled at her and told her that grounding a kid for walking up to the store and missing all the action seemed a bit much to me. Besides, any consequences I might have would certainly pale to the consequences they had already received.

By week's end, she had recovered as only teenagers can. She and her friends were so busy doing what young people do that the trip to Florida seemed all but a distant nightmare.

It was a hard lesson for my daughter and her friends to learn. Life will not always be fair, just, or responsive to the truth. The girls paid a heavy price for the boys behavior while they got to throw up on the beaches for the entire week.

I know that we will share many laughs about this episode in years to come. For now, I'm just glad to see the girls recover so well.

It's funny that this should all come about during Easter week – a time that people celebrate the resurrection of life. I have learned long ago that when it comes to resurrection from the dead, no one does so better than teenagers.

CHOOSING A COLLEGE III

And The Winner Is ... Or Isn't

My daughter tends to procrastinate better than most. She's a very laid back, easy going young lady who possesses a solid reserve of patients. Though she is a very friendly, out-going person, she is not the kind of person that you can sit down with and engage in any deep, complex conversations. Though you trust that she is planning for her future, you never quite know just how she is going about it. And yes, I admit that those who know me would follow these comments with a dumbfounded, "Gee, Andy, I wonder where she gets that!?" When it comes to swimming in the gene pool, she is definitely daddy's girl.

Going through the tedious chore of choosing a college has been a bit of a lesson in panicked anxiety for this inexperienced father. Every time I asked her where she stood in the great hunt for the perfect baseball cap... what school she was looking at... who she was talking to... hey, any shred of information that she could share with me... was always met with a casual, one line reference to everything being just fine and that I was not to worry about it.

But worry is what parents do best, especially when it comes to making decisions that may have a profound affect on my ever- thin wallet.

The phone rang constantly.

Every week, coaches would call to find out how she was doing.

Alumni and students would call to see if she had any questions or if they could help her out with her decision.

Being the dad of course, I always got the follow up questions.

"Who was that?"... "What did they say?"

"Oh, it was just so-'n-so, from such-'n-such university. Just checking to see how I was doing."

"Yea, well, what did you tell them?"

"Not much. Just told them how I was doing in track."

Only my daughter could reduce a twenty-minute conversation on the phone to an uneventful news bite.

This has been going on for a month or so, and being my first time traveling down this road, I wasn't quite sure if there was something I should be doing to help matters along. I felt very awkward and clumsy.

Keep in mind that, being the fine student that I was, I only got calls from universities just checking to make sure I wasn't thinking about going to their college. I believe it's called quality control.

Anyway, I had the silly notion that there would be many late night episodes of weeding through the piles of brochures, booklets, maps and checklists. Long hours of making out pros and con lists for each school and checking it twice, to see which ones would be naughty or nice. Gathering up all the information to figure out just which one would best serve my daughter (and my wallet of course), for the next four years.

In all fairness to my daughter, I must admit that my earlier counsel of location, school colors and mascots did not exactly entice her to run to me for any further counsel on the subject. Though I have gallantly tried to redeem my reputation and encouraged her to feel free in discussing these matters with me, she has understandably kept dear old dad at arms length.

But time was running out. May 1st was the signing deadline and we were already half-past April. I really felt compelled to sound fatherly.

"I know you're a busy kid and all, but you do understand that you only have a few more weeks to decide on the college you're going to."

"Oh, dad, stop worrying. I've already decided."

"You've already decided? Were you planning on telling any one?"

"Sure. I already told the coach. All I have to do is fill out some forms and I'll be set."

Something inside me appreciates the fact that I do not own an assault rifle.

"I realize that I am only your father, dear, but colleges have this funny thing about being paid to educate young people like you. Don't you think that I should have had a small say in the matter?"

"Oh, dad, it will all work out. The coach already knows you're broke. She's working on getting me a job on campus to cover what the scholarships don't. Don't worry about it."

The coach already knows I'm broke.... gee, how comforting! And don't worry about it? I have a moral obligation as a father to worry about it. After all, I have a long history of slick salesmen telling me that it will all work out and not to worry about it, only to find myself a few months latter wondering how the hell I got into such a financial mess. Don't tell me not to worry.

But given a few days to simmer over it, I began to realize that my daughter is not only right, but doing exactly what dear old dad instructed her to do.

From the start, I have told her to follow her heart. Don't listen to the others, and certainly, never let money dictate your future. It was a decision that would have a great impact on her future and I really wanted it to be her decision to make. And so she has, just as I asked her to.

We made plans to travel north some 600 miles and

check everything out and finalize the deal. Everyone was excited, though the thought of my baby being so far away was starting to give me a sinking feeling in my heart, I admit.

We set aside a couple of days for the trip and headed north. As a city boy who grew up on the sunny beaches of San Diego, I fully understand that I haven't a clue as to what the attraction is to spending your life working down on the farm. This trip did nothing to resolve the issue. For what seemed to be an eternity, we drove through endless miles of neatly packaged rows of green stuff. The only thing I could be assured of was that for the next four years, my daughter would have plenty of corn on the cob to eat.

As we reached our destination, we were excited and nervous. This was a big step and the long, uneventful journey did nothing to calm our fears.

We met up with the coach, who was a very nice young lady. She really went out of her way to make us comfortable. We spent a day meeting people and doing tours. Everyone was very nice. There was no question that the university was committed to their students and providing a positive educational environment for them. When all was said and done, we got back in the car and pointed it through the cornfields towards Nashville.

The first one hundred miles or so was very quiet and uncomfortable. The only conversation was the token conversation one has when avoiding what really needed to be said. Being the parents responsibility in a situation like this to cut through the bull and get to the heart of the matter, I finally decided to break the ice.

"You know, your dad is a funny guy. When I think of a university, I always think of those big campuses they show you at half time during football games. I didn't realize they made universities that small."

The token short response by my daughter told me that I was on the same page as her.

"You know, there is a lot to be said for the smaller universities. They say you can get a much better education there. And these people seemed really nice and anxious to help you out."

Another short, token response convinced me to cut to the quick and get to the heart of the matter.

"You know, kid, there are no laws that say you must stay with your decision. If you have any reservations, it really is okay to back off and take another look at things."

For the next four hundred miles or so, we worked through the issue. By the time we saw the wonderful skyline of our Nashville home, we knew that for now, we had seen our last corn field.

It was very tough for my daughter to call the coach back and tell her of her decision not to attend the university. The coach was really a nice lady and my daughter really did feel like her track career would be in good hands with her. But track was not her life, and this was much too important a decision to make with any reservations.

We would always wonder how things would have

turned out had we given the small university a chance. But that's life. We spend half of our lives making decisions, and the other half wondering how things would have turned out if we had made the different decision. You simply can't beat yourself up worrying about stuff like that. We made the decision, and I, as her father, feel comfortable that it was a good decision.

Later, she would ask me what it was about the university that made me change my mind about it.

I smiled and winked at her. "I didn't care much for their baseball caps." She rolled her eyes as only a daughter can.

It was a tough episode, but we had worked through it and were now getting our lives back to normal.

SENIOR PROM

Learning the Art of Overkill

We live in a society where overkill is the only language we understand. We took something as silly as Sadam Hussein and produced a Gulf War of such magnitude that many of us still believe that President Bush had an open line to Steven Spielberg.

Hollywood won't even look at a script nowadays unless it has 'BLOCKBUSTER' written all over it.

I think every cable channel proclaims itself America's #1 sports station... every weatherman is America's favorite... and certainly, every show is the television event of the year.

The media is quick to turn news stories that are not all that newsworthy into soap opera headlines. We normal people are dismayed, as we realize that we will, once again, have to endure yet another made-for-tv movie about such worthless news items as some lady who cut her hubbies crown jewels off because he was an idiot. We will be told that this is important stuff that we need to see.

And I won't even get started on today's talk shows. Talk about overkill. No one can take the misery of the few poor souls at the end of the I.Q. scale and turn it into an issue of worldly importance better than today's talk shows.

We just can't be satisfied unless everything we do, read or see comes with monumental consequences, which, if I may say so, most of the time does not.
How did we get this way? Why can't we maintain a more reasonable perspective about the events of our lives? Why does so much have to be made out of so little?

Where did we go wrong?

Ladies and gentlemen, I give you the senior prom.

I believe that the first step in learning the fine art of overkill comes with the senior prom. Oh sure, you could argue the merits of many other events in our lives as the origin of such anxiety glut, but I dare say that the senior prom pales the competition in the wondrous world of super hype. Whether you are talking about my senior prom in 1970, or my daughters here in '94, the senior prom pretty much has remained the same from generation to generation.. too much over too little.

Long before the summer tan begins to fade, seniors are already talking about this year's senior prom. The hype and pressure is well established by Halloween and will turn to a raging forest fire soon after the holidays. It is an on-going soap opera that will lead even the best of parents to keep Dr. Kravorkian's phone number on their short list.

First on the list is of course, who to go with. Be it my generation or my daughter's, this issue pretty much falls into three groups.

1- Those that already have steady steadies. They don't have to worry about who they are going with. They only have to worry about the other pressing issues as what to wear, where to eat, transportation and generally doing everything just right so that they will truly be the envy of all royalty on that one evening.

2- The many that fall in and out of relationships as only teenagers can. One week, they are the talk of the town, the next week; the guy's a flea-bag scum who makes Charles Manson seem like an attractive fellow. The key to this group is timing. You certainly don't want the prom to arrive at a time when you are in contempt of the male chromosomes. That is not a good scenario. The pressure becomes enormous, especially if you come out of the holidays with a love life that is on shaky grounds. Do you hang on to the bum until after the prom, or dump him now and give yourself enough time to fan the flames with someone else?

Young people in this category may have several dates for the prom during the course of the year. It's kind of like those great football games that I use to love to watch where the team that won was always the last team to have the ball. Your date for the prom will simply be the one fellow who happens to be in good standing at the time.

3- There are those who have no love life, no prospects for a love life and possibly could care less. These people pretty much see the senior prom in the same manner that we adults see turning forty. We know it's out there. We know it will happen no matter what we do to avoid it. We dread its arrival, and pray that we can simply get through it with as little damage to the ego as possible.

The seniors begin the year with that one date firmly etched in their souls. That one date that will become the main focus with each other event that passes by. That one date that truly comes as a no-win situation. The hype, the pressure and the grand expectations will never embrace reality, yet to miss the blessed event would be the unforgivable sin of the senior. With the date issue going on through the course of the year, there are many other issues that the senior needs to deal with in pursuit of the perfect senior prom. I will take them in no particular order and, of course, speak in as general terms as a parent possibly can.

Dress codes: As a man with a house full of ladies, let me say this. I am the first to admit that women are by far the superior animal in our wonderful food chain. But when it comes to overkill events like the senior prom, the guys clearly are living on easy street.

After all, a tux is a tux, is a tux. You just rent the thing, wear it to the prom and return it the next day. You not only don't worry about some other guy wearing the same tux, you pretty much expect all the guys to look the same as you. If you want to show a little style, you wear red tennis shoes or some goofy bow tie.

Not so, the ladies.

The issue of what to wear to the senior prom is clearly the most important decision a woman will make in her lifetime, or so they lead us to believe. It ranks right up there with every other decision they have ever made in their lifetime. And speaking as a man who admits to having very little understanding about the subject, the pressure seems to be enormous for the ladies. You must, for instance, find a dress that is fashionable and in line with todays woman, yet, be careful not to show up at the prom wearing the same dress as anyone else. This requires a great deal of networking that men simply don't get. That's why they seem to go in packs to the mall when shopping for prom dresses.

Of course you also have to get through your parents, especially dear old dad who will never understand, no matter how you try to explain it, what the value is in spending $200 bucks for a dress that you wouldn't be caught dead in a second time.

"Why don't you wear that dress you wore to the senior prom?" will always be one of the worst comments a young lady could hear, bringing with it more tears than zits on Saturdays, spats with boyfriends, bad hair days, or the break-up of the Beach Boys!, (actually, I threw in the one about the Beach Boys in my ever constant attempt to try and relate to these things).

There are many other issues involved in planning your senior prom. They may pale to the issues of who to go with and what to wear but nevertheless, they are of great importance to this great process of overkill.

Transportation: Do you have access to a fancy car? Do you go in with others and rent a Limo? Dinner? Flowers? And of course, how will all this elegance be paid for? (behind every senior is a parent mumbling, "Well, maybe she'll get a bunch of scholarship money for college. Certainly, we can dip a little into her savings to help out. After all, it is her senior prom!").

All this planning, anticipation and anxiety from the first day of school finally reaches its moment of truth. The electricity generated from that one day of fragmented nerves is enough to light up a generation of Super Bowl halftimes.

Again, I am by most accounts, a male, and I fully admit that I just don't get it. How could I? Heck, the guy picks up his tux sometime during the day, takes a shower about an hour before he needs to pick up his date, swings by and picks up the flowers on the way to her house. The only real challenge is in getting the tux to fit right, which of course, they usually can't and simply give up trying after about ten minutes.

On the other hand, the young ladies have a well planned out agenda that damn near starts before sunrise, and rushes to a frantic state of panic by four o'clock, when the boy, who started getting ready at three, stands at the front door smiling and thinking that he looks cool, even though it is generally accepted that teenage boys were never created to wear a tux.

I will not pretend to explain how this all works out because, as is the case so often, I am just the dad and dads seldom have a clue. On that day for some reason, nails, hair and gussying up takes a good ten to twelve hours to achieve. I just found a baseball game on TV and waited for the several, tearful, exclamations, "Dad, you have to run down to the store and pick up....!"

Several pictures later, the glowing couple is out the door and headed for an evening of Cinderella elegance.

There is an uncomfortable calm in the house. The other ladies sit around in a glazed sigh with romantic commentary bliss, while I thumb through my TV Guide to see just what game it was I was trying to watch.

But the real meat of the story doesn't come until the next day. With everyone gathered to hear all the glorious details, the response becomes the same response that seniors have made for generations.

"Oh, it was okay."

After months of preparations...months of anguish over what color to paint your nails... countless hours of negotiations with an unreasonable dad over a $200 dollar dress you wouldn't be caught dead wearing a second time... the concerns over transportation, flowers, dinner, and everything else... it all boils down to this; a shoulder shrug, a crinkled nose and unconvincing "Oh, it was okay"?

The truth of the matter is that the senior prom, in all its hype and anticipation, is still only a dance. Few of the boys will sweat out the starch in their tux on that dance floor. And the young ladies will take more interest in checking out everyone else's dress, hairdos, and nails, than getting their starchy dates out on the dance floor.

My daughter spent about five minutes talking about the prom, and the rest of the weekend talking about the after prom.

I smiled a lot, as I realized that some things never change. I barely remember my senior prom, but I can still go on about the great fun we had at the after prom. I knew exactly what my daughter was talking about, which, with teenagers, is a most celebrated occasion.

We are a funny group of broken chromosomes. For months, we hype the prom with all its pageantry, elegance and magic. But when it is all over, we would rather talk about the after prom with its t-shirts, jeans and pizza.

No matter what generation you call your own, the senior prom story seems to always read the same.

For my daughter the prom was just some fancy dance that she and her friends left early to get the after prom party cranked up.

For dad, there is the calm and peace in knowing that all negotiations are over. The deed is done. You take pleasure in knowing that she got through it without any disasters. A pleasure that is short lived when she announces, "Gee dad, you know graduation is only a few weeks away and you know I'll need a new dress for that!"

"Two hundred bucks for another dress that you will cover with a cap 'n gown?"

Yes some things never do change.

Talk about overkill and you certainly have to start with the senior prom. At least for the ladies.

Guys just don't over kill like women, although my lovely wife calmly reminds me that with only a few minor changes, this story could have easily been written for one Super Bowl Sunday.

Well I'm offended, but then she just doesn't understand about the Super Bowl.

But I'll never get out of that one alive.

I'd be well advised to quietly find another baseball game on TV.

NHS

The Chord Says More Than the Evening News

I PLEDGE TO MAINTAIN MY HIGH
SCHOLASTIC STANDING
TO HOLD AS FUNDAMENTAL AND WORTHY
AN UNTARNISHED CHARACTER TO ENDEAVOR
INTELLIGENTLY AND COURTEOUSLY
TO BE A LEADER AND GIVE MYSELF FREELY IN
SERVICE TO OTHERS
IN DOING SO, I SHALL PROVE MYSELF WORTHY
OF A PLACE
IN THE NATIONAL HONORS SOCIETY

It's just a simple yellow chord they place around your neck at graduation. Most people do not understand what the yellow chord represents. Heck, I would guess that most people don't even notice. But to me, that yellow chord represents the answer.

We turn on the evening news every night and watch in horror of stories about guns and violence that has reached even into our children's schools.

We clamor for answers.

We see a world of chaos with countries raging internal wars of brother against brother, tribe against tribe, religion against religion, in some of the most inhumane acts of hatred ever witnessed.

We cry out for answers.

We see a fragile world of ecological imbalance, brought on by selfishness and greed.

We reach for answers.

We see disease assaulting our bodies and our moral fiber, bringing far too many lives to an early end.

We pray for answers.

Domestic violence, drug abuse, alcohol abuse, sexual abuse, child abuse, consumer abuse, abuse of power, budget abuse, environmental abuse, abuse, abuse, abuse. After watching the evening news, we ask ourselves if there is any hope for this broken world that we have created.

But the answer will not be found on the evening news.

In high school gyms throughout the country, small, quiet ceremonies are being conducted. It is not well publicized, even at the schools. There is no pep band playing, no cheerleaders, and no long, boring speeches. It certainly does not generate the excitement that a football banquet does. There are no buckets of fried chicken, and you certainly do not have to worry about getting a good seat because like so many other events of this nature, only the parents of the children involved are present.

The ceremony only lasts about one half-hour. They say a few nice things and then call the kids up to receive their yellow chord. Yet with this very quiet, uneventful event, we can see the answer to many of those questions brought to us by the evening news.

These kids belong to the National Honors Society. The yellow chord they wear means that they have been wrestling with the toughest courses a high school can throw at them, yet they have mastered these courses with grades I could only hope for in PE. And there is more to these kids. You do not get into the NHS by sitting at home reading books and watching 'Return Of The Nerds'. You not only have to have the academic know how, you must be service oriented and a leader among your peers. These are the doers. These kids have balance written all over their resume. They know how to hit the good times as well as the books. And they know when to do both.

You can watch the evening news and wonder if there is any hope for tomorrow. But if you really want some answers, I suggest that you head to the nearest high school gym the next time they hold the National Honors Society Banquet. When you see these kids with the yellow chord around their shoulders, you will begin to see that the evening news doesn't really tell the whole story. They only tell the stories that sell. Yes, there really is plenty of reason to be optimistic about our future.

My daughter has a room full of trophies, plaques, ribbons and medals for her fine athletic achievements. I am extremely proud of those awards. But I can tell you without hesitation that my greatest pride will come when she walks down the aisle on graduation day with that yellow chord draped over her shoulder.

As a man, I may not have made a great impact in this world. Certainly not as much as I would have liked to.

But as a father, that little yellow chord tells me that I have contributed so much more to the world we live in. I have provided a young lady who will probably never be on the evening news.

I have provided a part of the solution.

I have provided a part of the answer for a hopeful tomorrow.

TAG-ALONG DELIMA

No Cloning Please

I know that the focus of this book has been my daughter's senior year in high school, and rightfully so. With the title being, 'HER SENIOR YEAR', I certainly have felt a mild obligation to concentrate on those subject matters that pertain to being a dad of a senior in high school. After all, my first born has reached a very exciting point in her life, and I thought it only right that I should take the time to jot down a few notes in the interest of good story line.

The operative word here though is 'first'. She is my first born. We are going through this marvelous adventure together for the first time. She is a rookie senior, and I am a rookie senior dad.

Her Senior Year

Though I have referred to events as being 'the last time', it is understood that it is the last time for the first time.

What about those poor souls that follows, however?

What about the kids that peer down the hall and take careful notes of how the old man handles each event so that they will be better prepared for negotiations when they are seniors?

Is 'HER SENIOR YEAR' everyone's senior year?

One of the toughest assignments for a parent is finding that middle ground between encouraging individual growth and maintaining common standards for all to play by.

Having three older brothers, I am certainly well qualified to understand this tag-along dilemma. I don't know how many times I heard teachers say, "Gee Andy, your brother never had problems with this subject." You don't know how many times I wanted to jump right back at them with, "Yea, well my brother couldn't screw up a double play as good as I can, so back off, buster"

My brothers were very popular and very involved. They showed a lot of interest in areas I had no interest in. One of my brothers was my hero. He was so cool – he was the first guy to get thrown out of school for wearing a Beatles hair cut. Being four years younger than him, I really ate stuff like that up. He was captain of the debate team, senior class president, and the man about campus. He was the big brother every kid wants. I worshiped the ground he walked on.

But that's the problem. I worshiped the ground he walked on, but had no desire to walk on that ground myself.

Their lives of politics, drama and band were great for them, but I just wanted to play second base. Sure, I too got into Beatle mania, but give me a Hawaiian shirt and Beach Boys tape any day, thank you.

We were individuals, and we understood that. We pretty much got along fine on the brotherly love scales. The problem was with the people 'out there' who constantly expected me to fit into the same mold as my brothers. It really can be a frustrating dilemma for a person.

So I can certainly understand and appreciate the other two young ladies of the house, who now face the challenge of following a sister who has a room full of trophies, plaques and honors. Especially during this, her senior year, when they must feel like excess baggage in a world full of excitement focused around the many events of their sister's senior year.

The good news is that the three girls have a strong reservoir of love for each other. Yes there have been some battles, as was the case with my brothers, but I don't think you will find anyone who will question the love between the Smith girls.

And if I may say so, they have had the luxury of being raised by an old man who has always been a strong advocate of walking to the beat of your own drum.

Her Senior Year

The girls will have no memory of dad whining at them, "Why can't you be like your sister?" In fact, they may recall several times when I would whine at them. "Hey, stop trying to be like your sister, and just be yourself"

You're talking about a guy who damn near missed the eighties. I had a strong aversion to the warm-up suit clad, French water bottle sucking, cliquish-talking, BMW driving yuppie crowd.

People who say that cloning will never happen, were not very observant during the eighties.

I have always pushed my girls to find their own voice and use it the best way they can without worrying about what the others may say or think.

Daughter number 1 is a great athlete... the best distance runner to have worn the green and white. She is a top scholar and one of the nicest people you'll ever meet.

Daughter number 2 is a dedicated cheerleader, a spirited soccer player, a top student, and one of the most compassionate, considerate people I have ever known.

Daughter number 3 is the one I can relate to the most. She entered high school following her two older sisters and their impressive resumes, much as I did following my brothers. Though she plays on the soccer team, and has the tools to do well, her interests are more off the field than the others. She is an excellent student and an award-winning artist. She can easily match her talents on a canvas with the talents of her sisters on the track and cheerleading fields. She is a determined, strong-willed young lady, who has a soft, gentle side that overflows with kindness.

I'm sure the younger two want to scream every time someone approaches them with, "Why don't you run like your sister?"

Boy do I know that feeling.

I am so glad that they have individual skills, talents and interests. I'm glad that HER SENIOR YEAR will not likely be their senior year. And I'm thrilled that all three truly appreciates the ground the others walk on but are more than happy to walk on their own ground, thank you very much.

That's the joy of parenting. You encourage them to love one another, celebrate each other's victories, cry on each other's shoulders and be there whenever the other is in need.

But you also encourage them to look for the beat of that drum that beats for them. Walk their own path. Climb their own mountain. Hold up their own light to shine bright.

We, as a family, truly celebrate this, her senior year. But there have been many times when a reassuring hug is called for with the younger ones to let them know that their lives, their worlds, are just as celebrated.

Of course, I'm a soft touch. With these three young ladies, I'll take any excuse for a hug.

AWARD BANQUETS

Some Are Missing the Message

Award banquets at the high school level have become pretty generic. As is the case in so many other school functions, it is the parents who bring the salads and have done the most in raising money for all the trophies, plaques and lettermen jackets. We don't complain, however, because we have some eleven years experience of doing stuff like this without whining – as long as it helps out the kids. Besides, any parent loves to spend an evening sharing some good food with other parents and friends while the coach gets up and makes a fuss about your pride 'n joy.

I was a little more reflective at this banquet, being that – yes, I'm going to say it – this was going to be her last awards banquet. But it got me thinking about an issue that has been bothering me ever since I started hanging around my daughter, the athlete.

Trophies and plaques are nice. Recognition for athletic achievement is great, certainly. I possibly appreciate it more because I know how much work it takes to be consistently bad at a sport. I can only imagine how much more work, concentration and dedication it must take to perform at a level that garners the recognition these kids receive tonight.

But as I have come to know many of these kids over the past several years, I can't help but come away with another thought.

For the past four years, I have seen countless stories of athletes who graduate, many from some of the finest educational institutions, unable to master the simple task of reading a story. I've heard scores of interviews with strapping, huge athletes unable to speak in complete sentences. I don't know how many times I've heard athletes use awful grammar. Many have only mastered a goofy wave and 'Hi, mom' in front of a camera.

Over those same four years, I have been to countless swim meets and track meets. I have seen several young athletes sitting in the stands working on their homework as they wait for their next event. I have seen kids working in pockets of subjects, with the back of the bus hammering out math problems, the middle of the bus trying to solve science theories, and the group towards the front quietly reading their English Lit assignment.

I have heard several coaches bark at their athletes that if they have the discipline and concentration to be a champion in the pool, they have the discipline and concentration to be a champion in the school. My daughter has had coaches that followed her report card closely and maintained a strict policy that if your grades were not good, you did not participate.

So I ask myself how is it that I keep seeing these stories about athletes getting diplomas without being able to read them? Athletes who are unable to make it in their sport at the professional level, yet having no tools to make it anywhere else. How can this happen?

I think that the high profile sports and their coaches should take a few lessons from the other coaches of the less 'profitable' sports.

Athletes should be getting a strong message from the very first day that if you have the tools to be a winner on the field, you have the tools to be a winner in the classroom.

There should never be an exception.

There simply are no excuses.

And what bewilders me the most is that, in all do respect to my daughter, she is a runner. She has no game book to memorize. There are no assignments that she must instantly respond to as soon as the quarterback barks out an audible. She does not have countless game situations that she must be ready to react to quickly and correctly in order to excel in her sport.

She runs around a track, after all.

Yes, she has a strategy to use her pace and her competition to her advantage, but there certainly is no game books involved, here.

I have no idea how these strapping young athletes can master a complex play book and have the intelligence to be able to react instantly to every game situation, yet are unable to master any work in a classroom that they happen to pull up a chair in.

There simply is no excuse for this.

I'm a big sports fan, mind you. I truly look forward to the fall when I can sit back and enjoy a good football game. I am a baseball fanatic. And I have even become a bit of a basketball, hockey, well pretty much any competition is for the most part good for me.

I do not make a fuss over the money that professional athletes make. I think it's silly for people to make a stink over a slugger who makes three million a year for a job that requires a great deal of hard work and dedication, even during the off season, yet we say nothing about the actor who makes three million for a bad movie that only took three weeks of his time to ruin. Entertainment- good or bad- is entertainment, folks, and we always pay for entertainment.

But to let an athlete go through high school, then go through a fine university without the academic advantages that his diploma supposedly represents is inexcusable.

The coach of that athlete should be thrown off campus

with no questions asked. A coach should never be allowed on a campus unless he or she fully understands that an athlete certainly has the abilities to be expected to excel in the classroom as well as he does on the field. They should always be student athletes, and never just a big, burly mass of muscle.

I have certainly enjoyed watching my daughter participate in sports through the years, and am beaming with pride over the trophies, plaques and awards she has displayed in her room. But as a parent, I greatly appreciate the fact that her coaches through the years have made it clear to her that it was more important for her to be a winner in the classroom. What she does with her sport doesn't really matter. She has applied the determination and dedication so important in making her a champion in a competitive sport, to becoming a champion in the classroom as well. She has learned that if she can become a winner in a competitive sport, she can become a winner at anything else she applies herself to.

I just feel bad for the athletes. They, unfortunately, never got that message. They have been told all along that they were big and strong, but no one ever told them that they were intelligent, too.

What a shame.

What a waste.

It was yet another night of fried chicken, jello molds and brownies while listening to coaches shower your child with wonderful stories of accomplishments, and of course,

Dad's tears rolling down his macho cheeks once again in public. I never get use to it.

But to me, the real accomplishment is that my daughter achieved all this and will be walking the stage with the yellow chord around her shoulder to remind everyone she was truly a student/athlete.

BACCALAUREATE

―――――

Time To Pause and Say Thank You!

At first glance, Baccalaureate seems to be the square peg in a world full of round holes. It just doesn't fit. As we come down the final stretch leading to graduation, the menu is full of exciting events with recipes of fun, laughter and plenty of celebration. Baccalaureate comes off as the vanilla ice cream in a world of adventurous flavors.

Many of the students and their families don't even show up for the thing. The others do so because they are the kind of people who don't want to miss any moment that has anything to do with their child's graduation.

That's too bad.

Many people think that Baccalaureate is a religious

thing that is set aside for those who are into that sort of thing.

That's too bad, too.

Simply put. Baccalaureate is the pause button on the senior's fast-paced video of life.

For the senior, it is a time to put the party machine on hold and take a few moments to reflect on what they have accomplished over the past twelve years. It's a time to reflect on the many sacrifices and all the support of their parents, family and friends that has brought them to this point in their journey.

For the parents, it is a time to put down the checkbooks, buckets of chicken, pennants and pom-poms, and reflect on what they and their children have accomplished over the past twelve years.

It is a time to put all the fanfare and celebration to the side and focus for a moment on two very special words...

THANK YOU

In this rat-race world of rush, rush, rushing to keep up with the Jones, where the negative, seedy side of life dominates our headlines, talk shows and evening news, 'Thank You' certainly gets low mileage in today's world of information highways.

Baccalaureate is the time set aside for all of us to pause and simply learn how to say thank you again.

As a parent, how many times have I slammed a door, steaming to myself that a simple thank you would be nice for all the crap I have to do for her?! How many times did I feel completely unappreciated and that my daughter must think that I have absolutely no life other than hers? A simple 'thank you' from time to time would have certainly cooled a few flames.

On the other hand, I am quite confident that my daughter has often felt very frustrated with the old man as she tried to pursue those many adventures that I always encouraged her to go for, yet gave her nothing but grief along the way.

"We can't afford that!"

"I've got to be there, when?!? Why can't they do these things at a more convenient time for me?!?"

"You mean it's tonight!?! They should know better than to schedule this on a Monday night!?! For crying out loud, don't they know that my Chargers are playing the Raiders!?*!?"

I am certain that as a parent, I have missed far too many opportunities to say thank you to my daughter for all the wonderful activities and adventures she has brought into my world. Yes, even those that fell on Monday nights.

When you go to the park, you can always find a young mother telling her child to go back to the nice man and say thank you. We get off on the right track, but somehow along the way, we seem to get far too busy to remember those lessons that mother taught us at the park when we were youngsters.

A simple thank you note to family and friends who have shown kindness has become such a tedious chore for us. How sad.

A counselor once told me that she noticed that every time someone complimented me, I would always respond by making a joke. She suggested that it was impossible for me to accept a compliment without making a joke out of it.

"If someone gives you a compliment, why can't you just look at them and say thank you? Why do you have to make a joke? It's just a cute way of calling them a liar, if you ask me."

That was many years ago, but as you can tell, it still shoots right through my soul – probably because she was absolutely right. Even though I have worked hard through the years to become more sensitive to people when they compliment me, I must admit that it is still uncomfortable to simply look at them and say 'thank you'.

I'd still rather make a joke.

"I love you" is the most powerful phrase in any language, in any culture, and in any religion. Unfortunately, it is a phrase that has been much over used, watered down and far too often made synonymous with people, places and things that it should never have been connected with.

'Thank you' are the two words that give "I love you" its power.

When you say thank you, you are saying I love you in its purest form.

I'm glad I went to Baccalaureate. It reminded me that

good parenting isn't found by throwing money and material goods at the children, but by teaching them by your examples that the best way to express your love for them is simply by taking a moment to say thank you.

It was a time to push the pause button on all the excitement of being a senior dad, as I quietly, and admittedly tearfully, gave my daughter a hug and simply said 'thank you'.

I just don't think you can say 'I love you' to your children any better than that!

GRADUATION DAY

Mixing Tears of Joy and Sadness

Being a man, there is always that dreaded macho stigma hanging over you that a 'real' man never shows his true emotions. I think fatherhood pretty much sinks that ship, and thankfully so. I have become quite use to the idea that I have never been, nor shall I ever be a 'real' man.

I'm a softy, okay.

How many times have I panicked as the lights began to come up at the movies while I was still frantically trying to wipe the tears from my eyes over another touching love story?

I remember how embarrassed I was as a youth when I went with some friends to see 'The Music Man' and desperately needed a hanky at the end.

Her Senior Year

I have always been a soft touch for musicals. Not too many real men would say that, I suppose.

So call me a fraud of manhood and see if I care. I love stories that are tender, romantic and sweet. If that causes me to be banned from membership into the brotherhood of man, so be it.

And when it comes to my kids, forget it! I'm a basket case from the start. Holding back my tears in a humble attempt to preserve my manhood, be it at banquets, recitals, or performances, is a hopeless chore I have given up on a long time ago.

I remember at my daughter's last cross country meet when she beat the school record. She had a room full of trophies, plaques, medals and certificates for her achievements over the past four years, but the one thing she did not have, that she wanted the most, was the school record. She wanted her name up on the gym wall proclaiming her the fastest distance runner in the school's history.

Last week, she had a great run, but came up four seconds short of the record.

Today would be the last chance for her.

There would be no more tomorrows.

I positioned myself away from the crowd, on the final bend where the runners come into view and head for the home stretch. If she wasn't going to get the record, it would break my heart. She had worked so hard and wanted it so bad. It was now or never, and a parent hates the emotional volcano rumbling inside as you stand on the sidelines, unable to do anything but watch. Especially in a race that spans some three miles. A race that lasts some nineteen minutes or more. A race in which a fair amount is run out of view of neurotic parents.

As the race progressed, things were looking fairly good. She looked fresh and focused. Conditions were perfect for her. It was cloudy and cold with snow flurries fluttering about. She always loved running when the conditions were bad.

She was my mudder.

The toughest part of the race for the parents was when the runners would disappear for about a quarter-mile until they rounded the bend where I was standing and headed down the home stretch. It was during this stretch where those who had it made their move, while those who didn't simply faded off.

As I anxiously waited at the bend, a few of the girls made the turn and headed for home. They were the ones who always win these races and today would be no different.

I continued to pace, nervously watching my clock, then the corner.

Then it happened.

Around the bend came the familiar green and white that I had been following for the past four years. It was her. I looked at my clock and absolutely fell apart. She could damn near walk the rest of the way and still beat the record!

I started jumping and running beside her, screaming and yelling with excitement, as she remained focused and desperately trying to ignore the fool running along side of her. I'm sure she told everyone that she had no idea who that lunatic was up at the bend.

But everyone knew.

Only a Dad would behave that crazy.

You hope in a race like this that you might be able to beat the record by one second or so. Today my daughter beat the school record by a whopping twelve seconds!

Of course, unofficially, I smashed the worlds record for the high jump of fatherhood.

As her coaches, teammates and friends celebrated her achievement past the finished line, I laid on the ground alone, up by the bend, crying buckets of tears of joy, hoping that the cold weather would not turn those tears into a solid block of ice for this proud father.

Manhood be damned! Fatherhood always takes priority in my heart. This was not a time to be cool and collected. My daughter had just presented her school with a new record for young ladies to strive for in years to come. I had little concern for my manhood, or some silly image we call 'macho'. It will always go down as one of the greatest, most thrilling days of my life.

So as you can see, this was definitely one man who would be stocking up on tissue as graduation approached.

In light of my blubbering performance at Baccalaureate, the awards banquet and track meets, I just told people that I would be resigning myself to the way things are and simply tape a few sponges on my cheeks for graduation night.

A senior year can really ruin a manly image in a father, you know.

It's funny how things don't always turn out quite the way we expect them to.

Graduation night found me a bit on the mellow side. I was much less excited than I thought I would be. I thought maybe it was just another chapter of this overkill that we do so well. You build events like this up so much and then feel a bit let down when the event arrives and we realize that it is, after all, just another event in this busy world full of events that we have come to call a life.

The ceremony was nice. Everything went off without a hitch. There were nice speeches, just enough pomp and circumstance to give it a royal flavor, but not too much. And of course there was the long chore of trying to recognize each student as they walked across the stage to receive their diploma.

Hey, for the past several years, these kids have been recognized by the individual clothes and personalities, and now they are killing us by making them all wear the same thing and behave in the same manner on the most important day of their lives. The wife and I, as I'm quite sure every other parent there, found ourselves constantly turning to each other with that bewildered look and asking, "Is that the boy...?" We finally gave up by the time they got to the 'Fs'

But on this night, I found my thoughts and emotions being channeled in a different direction.

Instead of getting all worked up about my little girls graduation, I instead found my thoughts focused on the many friends who have played such an important role in turning our home into Grand Central Station over the past several years.

With each passing face down the aisle, I saw years of great memories. Some reaching back as far as grade school, while others having only made brief appearances in my life. But all provided a sigh full of memories. Some of the faces had become so much a part of my world, they were truly thought of as family. I found myself feeling a bit sad and disturbed.

Sure I celebrate my daughters' accomplishments and will always enjoy watching her grow through the many stages that will take her from teenager, to young adult, to contributing woman. I am very happy to say that I will always be a part of her life.

But as I proudly look into these familiar faces passing by, I can't help but think that I am being cheated. I suspect that there are other parents in the crowd that understand how I feel.

Yes, these are my daughter's friends, but hey, they have become my friends as well. Yes, they have provided many wonderful memories throughout my daughter's life, but they have also brought a lot of pleasure and laughter into my world, too.

Though I am certain that my daughter will continue to get together with many of these faces whenever the opportunity presents itself, I must face the reality that with the exception of only an occasional encounter from time to time, this will likely be the end of the line for me in their lives.

I just don't like the prospects of that, to be honest with you.

We have become a very mobile society. We move to new addresses and change jobs much more frequently than any other generation before us. Fiftieth anniversaries will quietly fade away as we celebrate twenty-fifth anniversaries with a sense of astonishment that a relationship could actually last that long.

This generation deals with so many relationships coming in and out of our lives that the older generations just shake their heads and wonder how loyalty and commitment will ever survive. Tonight, I understand how they feel.

Oh, how tonight I long for the days when everyone pretty much stayed close to the nest. Where kids would graduate, go to college, and establish their careers pretty much in the same zip code. Where the biggest move was the young man climbing on the train to join the service for the next four years.

As I look at all these smiling faces that have been such

an active part of my life these past several years, I can't help wishing that I could get my hands on a time machine.

But reality is reality, and tonight, reality doesn't look that good to me. The reality is that for many, the warm, embracing hugs I receive tonight may well be the last, as their roads take them down a path far removed from my own.

I truly am excited for all these kids.

Over the past several years, they have convinced me that the world will be in good hands if my generation is smart enough to let go and put it into the hands of these fine people. With each hug I received tonight, I knew that I was embracing the solution to many of the problems this crazy world has created.

I hope that these kids understand that they will always be welcome in my home. I hope that they feel comfortable enough to drop by from time to time, if only to say a brief hello to the old man, whenever they are in town.

But again, reality sinks in.

These are my daughter's friends, and I have always been, and will continue to be, in the role of the parent.

So as I reflect on this graduation, I can't help but feel a bit surprised. I was expecting to be a blubbering basket case watching my little girl make her final appearance as a high school senior.

Instead, I found myself a bit subdued and disappointed in knowing that this great night of celebration would also represent an unspoken farewell hug for many of the great young people that have been such a joy to know over the years.

Yes there were many proud tears of celebration for what my daughter had achieved over the past twelve years. I just wasn't ready for those tears to have to compete with the tears of sadness that came with each hug and smile of the friends who will likely no longer be such an active part of my world.

I guess that is the part of being a parent that I hate the most. You come to realize that you not only get very involved with your children, but you also get very involved with your children's friends. And like so many other lessons through the years, we come to understand that, as a good parent, we know the time will come when we must simply let go.

I celebrate my daughter's life tonight. With her life, I have had the privilege of celebrating the lives of so many others. I wish all these young people the best in the years to come, knowing that they have certainly given me the best of years looking back.

Especially in this, HER SENIOR YEAR.

CARPE DIEM

Knowing for Whom the Bell Tolls

Crossroads. There are several times through our lives when we reach crossroads in the journey. Contrary to some beliefs, life is not a straight and narrow road we travel. Life is not a smooth and easy road.

There are many crossroads.

We often change directions and head down different roads in our journey through life.

Sometimes the road becomes much smoother and scenic.

Other times rough and unpleasant.

That is what makes life such a worthwhile adventure. Nobody travels down the same road. There will be times when our road is an open highway with many others sharing the same path, and other times when the road seems like a dissolute, lonely dead end.

There will be intersections where others will pass through your life, some providing happy memories and others you will be happy to see fading in your rear-view mirror.

In this, *HER SENIOR YEAR*, we have reached one of the major intersections of life, where many who have traveled down the same road will be choosing between the off ramps and on ramps of life that will take them in many different directions.

But before we turn off and head down the new road, let's take a few moments to reflect on the road that we have been traveling. Let's put the brakes on and take a look back before we all wave and head down separate roads.

What is the point of *HER SENIOR YEAR*?

What does it all mean?

Do all these events that we have been through really mean any thing now that they are behind us?

Are all these events merely entertaining stories, or are there lessons to be learned that we can take with us as we turn off this highway and head in so many other directions?

From class rings, to senior pictures and first day of school. From football games to homecoming rallies, to senior talent shows. From track meets to banquets, to becoming a jock dad. From spring break, to senior prom, to Baccalaureate, and finally on to graduation. These events are much more than just something to fill our calendars with. These events were a lot more than just explosive fireworks that quickly faded away to make room for the next explosive event.

HER SENIOR YEAR is a lot more than a chronological essay.

I believe that the events we shared in HER SENIOR YEAR says a lot about who we are as a student, a parent and as a society.

I have certainly learned a lot about my daughter through the events that she has participated in.

I have learned a lot about myself as a father through the events of the past four years.

And I think we all have learned a lot about what kind of people we have become through the events of this, HER SENIOR YEAR.

Be it my daughter, myself, or we as a people, these events teach us one of the most important lessons we must learn in order to survive.

It is a word that seems to have taken a back seat in our society, but I'm not fooled. Again, the evening news is notorious for sensationalizing the dark side of our character, even though it only reflects a small percentage of what makes us the real society that we are.

Whether you want to talk about ecology, politics, human rights, families, religion, education, or anything else, the solution will always depend on this one simple word:

INVOLVED

One of my favorite writings that I like to think captures what I believe life should be all about was written by John Donne in 1624:

ANY MAN'S DEATH DIMINISHES ME,
BECAUSE I AM INVOLVED IN MANKIND.
THEREFORE, NEVER SEND TO KNOW
FOR WHOM THE BELL TOLLS,
IT TOLLS FOR THEE.

We can talk all day about the problems of the world, and produce volumes of reports and essays explaining in great depth what needs to be done in order to make our world a better place to live. But we will never reach solutions to any of our problems until we become involved.

Is my daughter ready to leave the nest because she is a great athlete? No.

Is she ready to take on the demands of college because she is so smart? No.

Is she ready to pursue her dreams because she wrote a nice skit for the senior talent show? Not likely.

My daughter is ready to leave the nest and pursue her own interests because she has learned to become involved.

Was she successful at everything she did? No.

Did she reach all the goals she set out to? Certainly not.

Does any of this really matter? Not really.

Her Senior Year

What matters is that she was involved. What matters is that she had the confidence to try new things and get involved in the many opportunities that her school provided her.

Am I a great father because I found the time to play taxi man for all these events? No.

Am I a great father because I cut back on many of the things I wanted so that I could afford some of the things she needed? No.

I am a great father simply because I got involved in my daughter's life.

The events of HER SENIOR YEAR is a lot more than a chronological collection of cute little stories. We can all learn from these events that success is never measured by how many goals are achieved or how much wealth is accumulated. A persons demise is not measured by the number of failures or lack of material possessions. The quality of a person must always be measured by how much they have become involved in the world that they have been given.

My daughter will be successful because she has learned the joys and the heartaches of becoming involved.

I have become a great father because I have learned that becoming an involved parent should never constitute an image of sacrificing.

And I can't help but think that the world will become a better place to live because most of us are much too involved with each other's lives to have much time for the evening news.

The roads we travel may not all be headed in the same direction, but as long as we remain involved with each other as well as our world, we should all pretty much end up crossing the same finish line.

My daughter has a sweatshirt from one of her favorite movies, Dead Poets Society. It reads, 'CARPE DIEM', which means, seize the day.

We will all make this a better world if we learn to seize each day and become INVOLVED.

Carpe Diem to us all.

FINAL THOUGHTS

Creating the Perfect Resume

How appropriate that I should sit down and put the finishing touches of this book on this particular day.

The past year has been an emotional roller-coaster ride for me in this, HER SENIOR YEAR.

I have gone through so many emotional peaks and valleys that my heart is ready to go on strike if I don't just find one emotion and stick with it. A heart really takes a beating on a year like this. I have shed so many tears, some from the wells of pride and others from the wells of feeling sorry for myself. I have embraced the feelings of sheer ecstasy and the pain of absolute frustration. My poor heart has been battered and broken, pumped up and sent soaring.

Now that the graduation gowns have all been put away

and the parties have all been reduced to a few extra trash bags in the back, HER SENIOR YEAR is now history. I feel good that I have documented every step of this great year. When a writer starts a new project, he always looks forward to the day when he can type out those two glorious words:

THE END

It's not that you don't enjoy the tedious chore of writing the book, but more that you, and hopefully many other readers to come, are anxious to find out how the story ends.

A writer is very much like a sculpture. You start with a story idea and begin to work with it like a clump of clay. You add some here, and trash some over there. You know the direction you want your story to go, but you're never quite sure how each step along the way will create itself and carry you to the next step. There is a greatly anticipated sense of accomplishment in reaching the point where you can sit back, look at the mound of paper and say, "It's done!"

And though I certainly feel a sense of accomplishment in putting on the final touches of this book, I am understandably much more appreciative of the subject matter in this case than I am the book, itself.

This is a nutty world we live in. There are no rhymes or reasons to many of our adventures. As we travel through this world and choose to bring children into this chaos we call life, I have come to believe that there are only two things that you should teach them;

1) SELF-DISCIPLINE
2) SELF-CONFIDENCE

Self-discipline helps you to become a responsible person. That is why parents create chores for their kids. Hey, if my girls are successful enough later on to have someone else come in and clean their bathroom, that's fine with me. Cleaning the bathroom, or any of the other chores, were never the issue with me. The issue was to learn how to do something that you do not particularly enjoy doing without having to be told to do so. The issue is taking responsibility for doing something you may not like doing, and doing a good job at it.

I'm sure my girls have grown tired of hearing my sermon about people who work at minimum wage jobs that do not survive long if they constantly stand around with their hands in their pockets waiting for someone to tell them what to do next. That's why parents are constantly yelling, "I shouldn't have to tell you to do that!" over and over again.

Self-discipline. With it, your child will develop a solid sense of responsibility that will fuel them no matter what road they choose to travel in life.

Self-confidence pretty much speaks for itself. In the history of mankind, there has never been, nor will there ever be, a successful person at anything without a healthy measure of self- confidence. A parent simply must encourage their children to believe in themselves. To believe that they can be successful at life. This message must begin at the crib and be consistent throughout their development.

Of course, you must be realistic. Nothing makes me want to throw up more than an over-praising parent. Nothing destroys self-confidence more than false praise. If the kid takes dancing lessons and has two left feet, you sure don't want to shower them with praise and tell them that they are destined to be the next Fred Astair. You encourage them by telling them how great it is to try new things, and that no one is successful at everything they try. That failure is not when someone is unsuccessful at something they try; failure only comes when you don't have the courage to try in the first place.

Self-confidence. Believe in yourself and you will find an exciting world out there that will believe in you also.

Self-discipline and self-confidence. If you want to raise your children to be successful in life, these are the tools that you must give them.

So as my first born prepares to leave the nest, I not only take great pride over all that she has accomplished, I also take a few moments to pat myself on the back with a heart-filled, 'job well done!'.

Being a writer of starving persuasion, I suppose there are many who would consider me much less than a successful man. I think it is safe to say that there is not many that point to my life and say, "Hey, now there's a guy who knows all about success."

At forty something, I have had so many odd jobs that even odd people think I'm odd, (after a year and a half working at the morgue, I can perform a good autopsy, if anyone cares!).

I have worked my tail off just so I could exist on a very watered down paycheck-to-paycheck lifestyle. I have dealt with so many bill collectors that I could probably start my own agency, (The Andy Smith Kick 'em While They're Down, Inc.). I am after all, a nice guy who has spent most of my adult life working my way up to zero. Everybody says nice guys finish last, and I have done nothing to prove them wrong.

I am a hopeless dreamer. I am a guy who is constantly reaching for his star and always seems to come up a few pages short.

A non-conformist.

One who walks to a beat of another drum.

Guilty as charged.

I am also certain that I will never be accused of being a very religious man. I'm far too opinionated. I never accept things just because others tell me it is so. If it doesn't fit right with me, I have no problem in challenging it. I am not afraid to rock the boat while others are quietly standing by in a posture of conformity.

But I will also say that there is probably not many other people who has more faith in God than I.

You don't travel down the road I've traveled without a firm belief that God is hanging in there with you. I'm honest enough to say that there have been many times when I felt like God was the only one standing with me.

I may well be the Dennis the Menace of the Lord's family, but I have a very firm belief that if you are an honest person and continue to put your best foot forward, God will always see you through.

We all spend a lot of time pondering the hereafter. Many people think that our goal in life is to gather up as many points as possible to secure your cozy mansion in the sky, as if life is nothing more than a glorified video game. They envision St. Pete standing there with a calculator adding up all your good deeds and subtracting all your infractions, while you wait anxiously to see if you made enough points to pass through them pearly gates.

I can't get too excited about that though. I guess if everyone started out at the same point, it might make sense.

But we don't.

Some are born into freedom and are able to follow their dreams, while others are born into a world of stifled dreams and dictated paths. Some will never know hunger, while others will have so few calories to count on. Some will always know the security of a strong, loving family, while others may never know what family is. I just can't bring myself to believe that Heaven is only reserved for the point gatherers in a world of such diversity.

Her Senior Year

When my time comes to turn in my dance card of life, I really don't think God is going to care about how much money I made. If I remember right, there was a guy some two thousand years ago who was very bright, articulate and certainly capable of bringing home some serious income, but died on a cross with no material wealth to show for his life.

I don't think Pete's going to make much of an issue in the career choices I have made. "You spent your entire life trying to become a writer, when God wanted you to be a plumber? You idiot! You really blew it, pal! See 'ya."

However, I do believe that if you choose to bring children into this world, God will be interested in how you handled the serious responsibility of being a parent.

In the eyes of society, I may not be an image of glowing success. No argument there. Being a writer can certainly be a frustrating, lonely road to travel, with many potholes and winding curves along the way. You always seem to be lost in a jungle of intimidating nonsense, never quite sure if the direction you are headed will lead you out of the jungle or even deeper into it's grip. It is the road I have chosen, and if I should remain lost in that jungle for the rest of my life, I will not complain. At least I will always know that I gave it my best shot.

But when Pete asks me for my resume of life, I will simply hand him a picture of my three girls.

I have contributed to this world three girls who are positive, happy, considerate and sensitive to others. They are hard workers and team players. They are well equipped with the self-discipline and self-confidence that I spoke about earlier. They will, no doubt, be a part of the world's solutions, not its problems. You just can't take with you a better resume than my three girls.

So it is only fitting that I should put the final touches on this, HER SENIOR YEAR, on this particular day.

Today is Fathers Day.

After all these stories about the many exciting adventures in my daughters senior year in high school, I think it is okay to look inward and give my heart a big high-five and say, "Way to go, pops!"

Most parents, I believe, spend a great deal of time focused on their children's world, and rightfully so. Every stage that leads into the next stage is a tremendous gift to be embraced and enjoyed. I have truly enjoyed the many events and opportunities I have had to be a part of during my daughter's senior year in high school. I really look forward to sharing many of these events again with daughters number 2 and 3.

Being their father is a privilege that I do not take lightly.

But a parent also needs to pause now and then to pat themselves on the back for the great contributions they have made to this world.

A little self-gratitude can be good for the soul, too.

As a writer, I am glad to be done with this book.

As a father, I am thrilled that the story does not end here.

Her Senior Year

The End

www.ingramcontent.com/pod-product-compliance
Lightning Source LLC
Chambersburg PA
CBHW021408290426
44108CB00010B/430